Tasting Paradise

Restaurants & Recipes of the Hawaiian Islands

SECOND EDITION

Karen Bacon

Coastal
IMPRESSIONS
PRESS, LLC

Tasting Paradise
Restaurants & Recipes of the Hawaiian Islands

Copyright © 2000 Karen Bacon
All rights reserved.

Cover art, illustrations, book design and production by Karen Bacon.

Maps courtesy of Wizard Publications and Karen Bacon.
Editing and proofreading by Betty A. Olson.

ISBN 0-9644327-1-4
Library of Congress Catalog Card Number 00-090364
Includes index.
Printed in China

Published by:
Coastal Impressions Press, LLC
Post Office Box 1006
Kula, Maui, Hawai`i 96790-1006
Fax and Phone: 808-878-3855
karenb@aloha.net

Please send any comments, questions or suggestions to the above address.

Grateful acknowledgment made to Pali Jae Lee and Night Rainbow Publishing Co. for permission to reprint the excerpts on page 11, from *Tales from the Night Rainbow*. Copyright 1988 by Pali Jae Lee and Koko Willis.

The author and publisher have made every effort to ensure that the information was accurate at press time; however, we assume no responsibility for errors or inconsistencies. While the sources of the information contained in this book are believed to be reliable, changes in price, days open, menu items, etc. are inevitable and are therefore not guaranteed.

*To Winnie, who is free to dance with the clouds, sing
with the wind and soar with the birds, may your spirit
fly high above these beautiful tropical islands where
you were always drawn to visit and never did.*

Acknowledgements

I offer my grateful acknowledgement to all the chefs and restaurant owners who have taken the time to contribute these recipes and participate in this project. Without you, this book wouldn't exist. I enjoyed many exceptional meals and express my deep appreciation to the chefs for spoiling me with such delicious and artistic food. To all of you in positions where you helped set up the dinners and accommodations, your graciousness and generosity is greatly appreciated! To David, my sweetheart, you always managed to adjust your schedule to accompany me on the adventure. Thank you for making the experience much sweeter, richer, and romantic. Cora, my beautiful daughter, once again you patiently watched and offered your support, growing expertise and valuable opinions, as I spent countless hours working on this book. Thank you! To Carol and Rich, thank you for your support, involvement, and belief in this project. It wouldn't have happened this way without you! To Betty, thanks for taking my stack of pages and improving them with your expertise. Barbara, thanks again! You are the original inspiration. Kevin and Kay, I appreciate both of you being there for Cora while I was traveling. To all my family and friends who have lovingly offered your support, belief and encouragement, I am grateful every day for the gifts that you offer. Chef James, thanks for sending so many books home with your guests and giving me a great story to inspire other chefs with the possibilities of Tasting Paradise. To Kaniela, thank you for sharing about the blessing with graciousness and humor. To all the greater powers that be and the beauty that surrounds us in Hawai`i, Mahalo. It is an honor to be here.

TABLE OF CONTENTS

A Chef's Perspective . . .

As a chef, I feel very fortunate to live and cook on a gorgeous tropical island that is known world-wide. I am passionate about the beauty and bounty that we chefs get to work with on a daily basis here in Hawai`i where there are countless great restaurants, many of which are featured in this book.

Over the last several years, we have seen a transition in the cuisine of Hawai`i that continues to evolve daily. There was a time when continental dining was the norm and the majority of produce was imported. That's not to say there wasn't anyone growing veggies for small markets and personal consumption and pleasure. There were. But fresh, unique island foods were not reaching mainstream visitors. Now—we the chefs, are networking with micro farms and aqua culture farmers and are able to deliver same day picked salads or fish directly to you, our guests. When the products are fresh and perfect, it is unbelievable! And here we are, chefs from all over the planet, with our different styles and knowledge, just having the time of our lives creating spectacular fusion dishes, as well as recreating traditional dishes using fresh island products. You get to enjoy the benefits of this when you visit our restaurants or try some of the recipes in this book that reflect this new and distinctive approach.

It isn't difficult becoming inspired to create unique dishes, when there are so many unique foods at our disposal. Think about this—a fisherman calls from his cell phone on his boat to tell you what he just caught and the next thing you know there's a beautiful fresh fish delivered at your front door. And then someone shows up with fresh picked avocado and star fruit. Well, you just chop up a Maui onion with that, and you have a fresh tropical salsa to put over that just-seared *papio*.

Life for the modern day chef isn't only cooking though. With so much popularity surrounding Hawaiian Regional Cuisine, we are often asked to go out and promote, and share our love with the rest of the world. In fact, I appeared on national TV with Karen Bacon to do a cooking demonstration when her last edition of *Tasting Paradise* was featured on the home shopping network QVC. Whether it's in the form of writing cookbooks, cooking at fund raisers, preparing menus for airlines, cooking abroad, cooking aboard luxury cruise ships, going on television and radio or doing joint cooking venues with other notable chefs, the bottom line is to do it with passion and consistency.

I hope that you will enjoy the recipes in this book and I look forward to saying *Aloha* to you in person.

Mahalo and a *Hui Hou,*

Chef James

Chef James McDonald is executive chef of I'o restaurant (page 116), Pacific'O restaurant (page 128) and The Feast at Lele, a fine-dining luau (page 104).

A Note from the Author

This project started with the adventure of travel and romantic gourmet dinners with wine, candlelight and ocean breezes. We sometimes even had two dinners a night! (So much food, so little time . . .) This led into months of long days and nights in front of the computer and at the drawing board, with only enough time to grab a tuna sandwich for sustenance. This is especially hard while writing about all of this phenomenal food! But completion is here and the end result is exciting and gratifying.

Many talented, creative people who are passionate about food and all that the Hawaiian Islands have to offer have contributed to this book. The selection of enticing recipes and restaurants represent the cultural diversity that Hawai`i is known for. As it adds a tremendous richness to be in a community where people of many cultures live together, *Tasting Paradise* holds a unique richness by offering a sampling of many different cuisines within its pages. This allows you to share in this cultural diversity while dining out in Hawai`i, and while creating in your own kitchens at home.

I invite you to try the delicious recipes, outstanding restaurants, and your own experience of *Tasting Paradise*.

Aloha,

Karen

Selecting the Restaurants*

A beautiful view, right on the beach, a unique and fun atmosphere, a lovely and elegant setting, a creative, innovative menu, great food . . . these are only some of the reasons that the restaurants in this book were selected. Most restaurants were recommended by word of mouth from people who live on the islands. I asked friends, friends of friends, restaurant owners, chefs and managers. Realizing that we all have different tastes, this book features a variety of restaurants with the goal that there will be something for everyone.

The type of cuisine for each restaurant is listed on the right hand side of the recipe page, followed by the town (or area) and island where the restaurant is located. Divided into sections by island, including maps, and with a complete recipe index, *Tasting Paradise* is easy to use as a cookbook and a restaurant guide.

The restaurant business is mercurial. There are often daily menu changes; therefore, when an item is mentioned in a write up in this book, it will not necessarily be on the menu when you arrive at the restaurant. Prices, hours and days open are subject to change. Owners, chefs and staff may also change, which can result in a shift in quality; a restaurant may close its doors and a new one will open in the same location. It's an adventure; be ready for surprises!

The Spirit of Aloha

Aloha means the spirit of love, and is commonly used as hello and goodbye; it also means compassion, kindness and giving.

> *Aloha* is being a part of all
>
> and all being a part of me.
>
> When there is pain—it is my pain.
>
> When there is joy—it is mine also.
>
> I respect all that is
>
> as part of the Creator and part of me.
>
> I will not willfully harm anyone or anything.
>
> When food is needed I will take only my need
>
> and explain why it is being taken.
>
> The earth, the sky, the sea are mine
>
> To care for, to cherish and to protect.
>
> This is Hawaiian—This is *Aloha*![1]

This beautiful message is from the book *Tales from the Night Rainbow*, by Pali Jae Lee and Koko Willis. The book was inspired by stories shared by their big grandma, Kaili`ohe Kame`ekua. As with all cultures, there are many different versions and interpretations of the history of the Hawaiian people. Much of what is commonly known is the history of the Tahitian people after they came to Hawai`i (the *Ali`i*). But the true native Hawaiians that were here before the Tahitians came (pre *Ali`i*) have a different history and philosophy of life. They taught through stories and parables that were shared with children at an early age, such as the two examples shared on this page.

> "Each child born has at birth, a Bowl of perfect Light. If he tends his Light it will grow in strength and he can do all things—swim with the shark, fly with the birds, know and understand all things. If, however, he becomes envious or jealous he drops a stone into his Bowl of Light and some of the Light goes out. Light and the stone cannot hold the same space. If he continues to put stones in the Bowl of Light, the Light will go out and he will become a stone. A stone does not grow, nor does it move. If at any time he tires of being a stone, all he needs to do is turn the bowl upside down and the stones will fall away and the Light will grow once more."[1]

As we experience the people and the spirit of *aloha* throughout the islands, it enriches our experience and keeps the history alive to share these stories and others like them.

---

[1] *Pali Jae Lee and Koko Willis, Tales from the Night Rainbow (Honolulu, Hawai`i: Night Rainbow Publishing Co., 1988), pp. 18–19.*

The Hawaiian Blessing – A Tradition

While the world is filled with people of different nationalities and cultures, religions and spiritual beliefs, there are things that tie us together—universal bridges such as food, which crosses language barriers, opens hearts, fills bellies and imparts a feeling of nourishment. In many cultures, we bless our food and ask for it to serve us well; we also bless our babies with hopes that the blessing will help them have a happy, healthy and successful life. We want our relationships to be rewarding and harmonious, our ventures to be successful.

In Hawai`i, it is a tradition to bless new homes, boats, canoes, and new businesses, including restaurants, calling upon greater powers to assist in the safety, well being and success of the new creation. The blessing also cleanses and clears the way of any conflict or bad experience that may have occurred in the past. The ceremony is performed by a spiritual leader—a *kahuna*, priest, *kahu* or minister— and reflects the individuals own unique style and philosophy. Friends, family and members of the community are drawn together to participate in the ceremony of honoring a new beginning.

"When getting ready to perform a blessing you must prepare to be strong in mind and purpose, enough to combat seen or unseen obstacles that might be before you, including personalities present," Kaniela Akaka, Jr., a Hawaiian historian explains. With inspired chants and prayer and the request for all who are present to clear their minds and think only positive thoughts for the restaurant, Kaniela performs a blessing, as he recently did for Alan Wong's new restaurant, The Pineapple Room. Kaniela explains that, for him, the chants are inspired in the moment. Each blessing is unique to fit the home or business it is for, and only with everyone's prayers along with his chants can the blessing and success of the restaurant be accomplished. Each person has a purpose and link to the whole; he relates it to a canoe voyage in which there are many roles and each one is vitally important to the success of the journey. In this case, the owner of the business is similar to the navigator who looks toward a goal, a guiding star. "We're all in this together and we need to work together and think as one. The restaurant, which is like a big canoe, needs everyone's helping hand—we will make it together. Each one of us is a part of this great wholeness," Kaniela says.

During the blessing, sea water is sprinkled on the four corners of the building or room, *pi kai* (salt) cleanses and purifies to clean out all the negative and unwanted elements, including what Kaniela refers to as "rascal spirits" who may make things hard. The prayers help the "rascals" move on and at the same time request other spirits who are present to help with their blessings. *Maile* (vines from the native Hawaiian shrub) are tied together to represent the *piko* (umbilical cord), or connection to the earth, which represents the mother. The *maile* is severed, as the umbilical cord is cut from the mother to enable the child to grow and move on without being held back. As part of the blessing, a lavish spread of food is presented—food that is a ceremonial feast, a commune with the gods, in which not only the physical world is invited to partake, but the spiritual world as well. The participants of the blessing are not only the witnesses of the event, but foster parents to help care for the new business—as there can be rough times, just as a canoe on a voyage can encounter rough seas or a child will go through challenging times. A blessing is a birth to a new spirit or life force and all who are there have the responsibility to help keep the life force alive.

As he begins his prayers and chants for the blessing, Kaniela asks for a feeling of love and *aloha* to bind everyone together as part of a family. He calls on spirits from the past to utilize the help of all considered part of nature and life, and they are invited to partake in the feasting—somewhat like a holy communion. He asks for silence, a conch shell is blown, and everyone brings their thoughts and *mana* (spiritual power) together as Kaniela and the owner of the new venture symbolically cut the *maile* and go from corner to corner sprinkling sea water as the blessing begins with the intention and awareness that our accomplishments will be much greater when we all work together as one.

Tasting Paradise is the result of many people contributing and working together to create a unique cookbook/restaurant guide for you to enjoy. It revolves around food, which is our lifeblood and, along with love, it nourishes us, brings us together and creates joy in our lives. Food is a creative expression, a way that we can share love and life with others; it is one of our greatest blessings.

Kaua`i

The Garden Isle

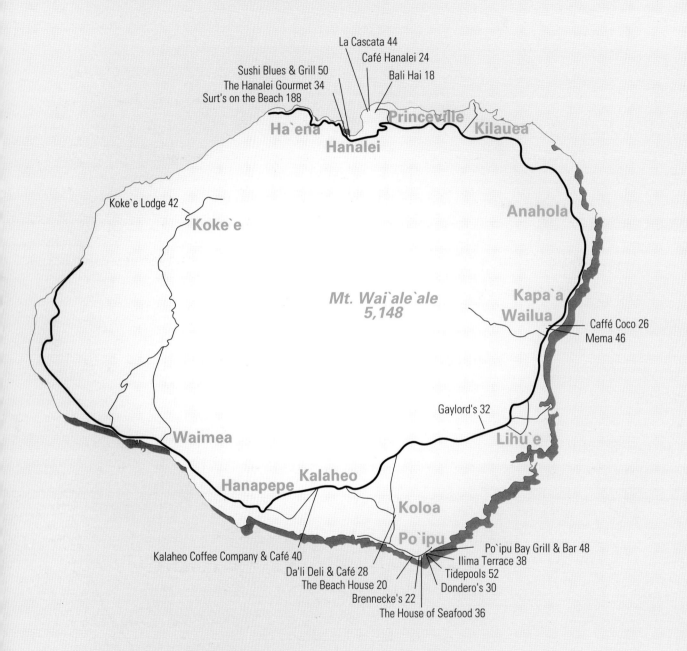

La Cascata 44
Café Hanalei 24
Bali Hai 18

Sushi Blues & Grill 50
The Hanalei Gourmet 34
Surt's on the Beach 188

Princeville

Kilauea

Ha`ena

Hanalei

Koke`e Lodge 42

Koke`e

Anahola

Mt. Wai`ale`ale
5,148

Kapa`a
Wailua

Caffé Coco 26
Mema 46

Gaylord's 32

Lihu`e

Waimea

Kalaheo

Hanapepe

Koloa

Po`ipu

Po`ipu Bay Grill & Bar 48
Ilima Terrace 38
Tidepools 52
Dondero's 30

Kalaheo Coffee Company & Café 40

Da'li Deli & Café 28
The Beach House 20
Brennecke's 22
The House of Seafood 36

Kaua`i

Restaurant, Page, Type of Cuisine
Recipes Featured

Hospitality, smiles, and aloha that comes from the heart—this is called ho`okipa and is part of the philosophy at **Bali Hai Restaurant** where the staff is taught about the Hawaiian culture to allow that special spirit to be shared with guests. In an open-air atmosphere that nearly surrounds you with majestic mountains and an exceptional view of Hanalei Bay and Bali Hai, voracious appetites for natural beauty and good food have plenty to devour.

Keeping the cuisine simple and fresh is important to the chef and is accomplished by using fresh Kaua`i produce and herbs that are organically grown in the restaurant's own garden. For a first course, try the Blackened Seared `Ahi with Cajun spices and a ginger wasabi beurre blanc; this is an outstanding combination, the sauce is dreamy and the presentation glorious. Several distinctive preparations

are available nightly for the fresh catch: Taste of the Kaua`i Rich Forest—pan seared, served over vegetables and laced with shiitake mushroom sauce; and Tropical Breeze— sautéed to perfection with a cool papaya, pineapple fruit salsa.

Breakfast items include Bay Benedict, Macadamia Nut Waffle and a variety of omelettes. Lunch features a soup of the day, some entrée salads and sandwiches.

Open daily. Breakfast: $6.00–12.50. Lunch: $9.00–14.00. Dinner: $18.00–32.00. Reservations recommended for dinner. Ask for directions from the Princeville entrance information booth.

MAHIMAHI BALI HAI SUNSET

4 mahimahi fillets, 4½ oz. each
8 squares puff pastry dough
1 egg, for egg wash
1 – 2 to 3 oz. portobello mushroom
1 oz. olive oil
1 clove garlic, minced
½ bulb shallot, minced
1 sprig thyme
¼ sprig rosemary

Filling ingredients:
1½ oz. boursin cheese
1½ oz. cream cheese
1½ oz. blue crab lump meat
1 tsp. capers
½ oz. red onion, minced
pinch of fresh rosemary, minced
½ oz. garlic, minced
½ oz. shallots, minced

Mix filling ingredients in a mixing bowl. Refrigerate for 15 minutes. Marinate mushroom in oil, herb, garlic and shallot mixture. Grill mushroom until tender but not mushy (3 to 4 minutes per side). Slice mushroom at an angle and set aside.

SWEET CHILI BEURRE BLANC

4 oz. white wine
1 oz. rice wine vinegar
1 oz. shallots, minced
1 oz. ginger root, peeled and mashed
juice of 1 lemon

juice of 1 lime
1 bay leaf
4 oz. heavy cream
¼ pound butter
4 oz. sweet chili sauce

In sauce pan, sweat shallots until translucent. Add white wine, rice vinegar, ginger root, lemon, lime juice and bay leaf. Reduce for 5 minutes over medium heat. Add cream and reduce by ⅔, being careful not to boil or scorch. Add butter slowly over medium heat. Turn off heat just before all butter is melted and strain. Stir in sweet chili sauce and keep in a warm place.

To assemble: Place 1 sheet of puff pastry on lightly floured board. Place 1 fish fillet on top of pastry. Top with ¼ cup stuffing mixture. Fan mushroom slices on top of stuffing. Take second piece of pastry (slightly larger than the first), egg wash edges and sandwich both layers together. Press out as much air as possible and pinch edges together to seal. Chill for 10 minutes in freezer. Place on oiled cooking tray. Brush with egg wash. Bake at 350 degrees for 20 minutes. Place on center of plate and spoon sauce around. Serve with sautéed vegetables.
Serves 4.

Executive Chef Androcles Handy

W hile sitting in an inviting open-air setting just steps from breaking waves, with a perfect sunset view over the glistening ocean, you can enjoy being seduced by the soft sounds and scents of the sea, gracious service and superb food. These elements combine to make **The Beach House** a uniquely special place to dine on the beautiful garden island of Kaua'i. A favorite restaurant on the island, The Beach House has been honored with the Hale 'Aina award for 3 consecutive years— 1998, 1999 and 2000, and has also received excellent ratings from *Zagat Survey*.

Now under new ownership, the restaurant continues to excel with the same core staff offering their talents including Executive Chef Linda Yamada who, honoring the natural spirit of food, brings great love, passion and creativity to her cooking. Manager Dana Higa infuses the team with a sense of family, heart and high quality standards, which add warmth and graciousness to each dining experience.

Enjoy the romantic atmosphere with a bottle of fine wine and a delicious entrée such as Seared Crusted Macadamia Nut Mahi with citrus aka miso sauce, or Mint Coriander Marinated Lamb Rack with goat cheese roasted garlic crust. Recommended appetizers include Sea Scallops with green papaya salad; and 'Ahi Taster—'ahi poke sushi, 'ahi tostadas and 'ahi hash spring roll. A dessert sure to please chocolate lovers is their Hawaiian Vintage Pyramid—a brownie nut crust with white chocolate mousse topped with chocolate fudge. Ooh la la!

Dinner served nightly. Entrées: $20.95–26.95.

Reservations recommended. When on Maui, visit sister restaurants, The Plantation House (page 130), and The SeaWatch (page 134).

CRISPY SESAME CHICKEN

4 chicken breasts

For marinade:
2 Tbsp. sesame oil
¼ cup soy sauce
¼ cup sherry
2 – 1" slices of ginger
2 pieces whole star anise
1½ Tbsp. sugar

For tempura:
1 cup cold water
1 tsp. sesame oil
2 eggs
1 cup all purpose flour
½ cup cornstarch
1 tsp. toasted white sesame seeds
1 tsp. black sesame seeds
½ tsp. baking powder

Mix all marinade ingredients together and let chicken breasts marinade for 24 hours.

Place water, sesame oil and eggs in a mixing bowl. Add remaining ingredients and mix slightly, leaving lumps. Over mixing will cause the batter to become heavy.

Roast marinaded chicken breast in oven for 15 minutes at 375 degrees. Remove from oven, dust lightly with flour and dip into tempura batter; fry until crisp. Place finished chicken breast on a bed of soba pasta, fried rice or tossed salad.

SEARED TOASTED MAC–NUT CRUST MAHI
WITH MISO CITRUS SAUCE

4 mahimahi fillets, 6 oz. each
salt and ground white pepper
½ cup unsalted butter, softened
¼ cup panko crumbs
½ cup toasted macadamia nuts,
    ground fine
2 Tbsp. olive oil

Miso Citrus Sauce:
½ cup dry white wine
¼ cup heavy cream
1 Tbsp. white miso paste
1 cup unsalted butter, soften and cut into cubes
1 tsp. lime juice

Season each fish fillet with salt and pepper. Mix the toasted macadamia nuts into the softened butter, add panko and salt and pepper to taste. Spread on top of the fish fillet with crust and sear quickly in hot sauté pan on both sides.

For Miso Citrus Sauce: In a sauce pan, reduce the wine by ⅓. Add the cream and reduce by another ⅓. Over a low heat, stir in miso paste, then slowly add butter, incorporating each cube. Be careful not to heat the sauce too high; sauce will break. Finish seasoning with lime juice, salt and pepper. Be careful with salt; miso paste is salty to begin with.

To serve, place warm sauce on plate with fish on top of sauce.

*R*ich blue sky, sparkling water, crashing waves, palm trees and people having fun in the sun; this is the view from **Brennecke's**. A South shore landmark, Brennecke's looks out over Po`ipu Beach Park from its second story open-air location. Bob and Christine French opened this popular restaurant in 1983, long before their daughter, Rochelle Ballard, became a world class surfer (Congratulations!). Look for the wall in the restaurant that is covered with photographs of her and the mighty waves. Bob and Christine opened Nukumoi Surf Shop next door, which is filled with great clothes and surf paraphernalia. Brennecke's, named after the world famous body surfing beach next to

Po`ipu Beach, is a great place to kick back, relax and have a cool one and a bite to eat. Try one of their "World Famous" Mai Tais or an icy pitcher of coladas, margaritas or daiquiris to share. The salad bar features a wide variety of items or enjoy an `Ahi Caesar Salad or Kiawe Broiled Catch of the Day. They prepare a daily salsa made with fresh fruit, such as: pineapple, papaya, mango, nectarine, and star fruit. Early dinner specials are offered from 4 to 6 p.m. (including a fresh catch) and they have a children's menu that features several kid pleasing selections. Full dinner entrées include Double Lobster Tails and Skewers of Shrimp, Ciopinno or Prime Rib. And, they have some killer desserts: Chocolate Suicide Cake and Suzie's Magical Mocha Pie. Lunch: $8.25–12.95. Dinner: $8.25–29.95. Open daily.

BRENNECKE'S "WRAP & ROLL"

FISH WRAP

1 – 10″ tomato wrap (or plain flour tortilla)

4 oz. fillet of fish (we use ahi)

¾ cup fine shredded cabbage

½ cup sour cream

½ cup corn relish or salsa

½ cup guacamole

The `ahi is (Kiawe) broiled, or you can cook it any way you like. Heat wrap on broiler or on gas stove top (not electric). Set wrap down. Cut fish into 5 or 6 pieces. Place cabbage in center of wrap in a line. Put fish on top of cabbage along line; top with relish and sour cream. Roll wrap tightly. Secure the roll with toothpick, if needed. Cut in half and cut one more time at an angle. Place in center of plate; stand two pieces on end and two lying down. Garnish with guacamole and tortilla chips. Serves 1 to 2.

If you prefer chicken, beef, pork or tofu—just substitute in place of fish.

BRENNECKE'S SEARED `AHI

¼ pound sashimi quality `ahi

½ cup teriyaki sauce

1 tsp. black sesame seeds

1 tsp. white roasted sesame seeds

2 tsp. furikaki

2 Tbsp. garlic oil

2 tsp. wasabi

2 oz. Nama ponzu

1 Tbsp. shredded red pickled ginger (optional)

½ cup finely shredded cabbage

Fish should be cut into a sashimi block. Marinate fish in teriyaki sauce for 1 to 2 hours, not longer. Heat garlic oil in small sauté pan. Heat it up very hot but not smoking. Sear `ahi very quickly on all four sides. Drain off excess oil. Mix furikaki with black and white sesame seeds; then roll seared `ahi until you coat all sides. Set up your plate with cabbage. Slice `ahi as you would for sashimi. Place on cabbage; garnish with pickled ginger. Mix wasabi with very little water until consistency of paste. Fill ramekin with Nama ponzu sauce and set wasabi to the side. Let each person mix to his/her own taste. Serves 1 to 2.

*E*njoying a meal on the terrace of **Café Hanalei** provides an unforgettable experience of elegance and grandeur with the set designers being both mother nature and human nature. The best of both worlds is laid out before you— verdant mountains crevassed with cascading waterfalls, the azure Pacific creeping into picturesque Hanalei Bay glistening below—and stately elegant architecture with exquisite attention to detail. Other places in the world, a hotel this grand and lovely could be pretentious, but on Kaua`i at the Princeville Hotel, the feeling of aloha prevails and it is comfortable and friendly.

The cuisine featured at Café Hanalei is a blend of different worlds and is created by Executive Chef Mark Secker who describes it as, "Pacific Rim cuisine with oriental overtones." Following an "East meets West" theme, he explains, "We work closely with local farmers who supply us with an array of homegrown products, including organic lettuce, taro and fresh herbs."

California Roll Sushi and Vietnamese Style Summer Rolls are wonderfully fresh for the tastebuds and colorful for the eyes. Entrées include an enticing combination of fresh fish selections, steak, chicken, and vegetarian dishes, all prepared in appetizing and unique ways. A light dessert with outstanding flavor is the Duo of Creme Brulée. (One is flavored with Kaua`i coffee, the other with ginger.) Cafe Hanalei features daily specials and signature dinner buffets, including Champagne Sunday Brunch and Seafood Buffet, which are absolutely incredible!

Open daily. Breakfast from 6:30 a.m. ($4.50–23.50.) Lunch is served from 11 a.m. to 2:30 p.m. ($11.50–18.95.) Dinner from 5:30 to 9:30 p.m. ($20.00–34.00.) Dinner reservations recommended.

CRISPY TARO ROOT PANCAKES

2 pounds fresh taro root (Chinese bong long)

4 cloves garlic, minced

4 Tbsp. grated parmesan cheese

½ cup whipping cream

1 egg

salt and pepper to taste

peanut oil and sesame oil mixed 1 part to 1 part for frying

Peel, quarter and grate taro root. Place in a stainless steel bowl. Add garlic, parmesan cheese, cream, egg and seasoning. Mix all of the ingredients until mixed well. In a teflon pan, add a small amount of the oil blend. Spoon taro mixture into hot oil and pan fry on both sides until golden brown. Remove from pan, drain excess oil and transfer pancakes to a baking sheet. Bake at 375 degrees until thoroughly cooked and crispy.

KAUA`I ONION SOUP

2 large Kaua`i sweet onions, sliced thin (may substitute Maui or Vaidalia)

4 Tbsp. olive oil

½ cup sweet Marsala wine

3 cups chicken broth or stock

3 cups beef broth or stock

salt and pepper

6 black peppercorns

3 cloves

1 bay leaf

croutons and cheese for topping

In heavy soup pot, heat the olive oil until smoking. Add the sliced onions; spread out but do not stir. Allow the onions to start to caramelize; then stir to expose all sides. When onions are well caramelized, add the Marsala wine and stir. When the wine is almost evaporated, add the stocks. Make a small sachet using cheesecloth and tie it up tightly with the peppercorns, cloves and bay leaf inside. Add to the soup; bring to a boil and turn down to simmer slowly for about 25 – 30 minutes. Adjust the seasoning with salt and pepper. Serve hot, topped with a toasted crouton and melted cheese.

Executive Chef Mark D. Secker

*O*f all the wonderful restaurants in Hawai`i, Caffé Coco is truly unique. It's as if stumbling upon a bistro in the middle of a jungle. An assortment of tables is gathered together on gravel under large umbrellas and awnings, with avocado and mango trees, surrounded by ferns, palms, flowering Bougainvillea, orchids, banana and ti plants. During the day the sunlight filters softly through the leaves and in the evening, tiki torches provide a warm glow accompanied by live music on most nights.

Owner/chef Ginger Carlson left her successful restaurant on the Mainland, retired, moved to Kaua`i and, with Sandra Jennings, opened Caffé Coco. As an artist, Ginger often painted bistro scenes that ultimately were the basis for this eclectic eatery. There are also some indoor tables that are situated in the artistically restored plantation cottage.

The service is extremely relaxed, so when you're there make sure you're on "island time." No worries; the food is fabulous. The creative menu changes often depending on what's fresh and available from local farmers and fishermen. There are many flavorful homemade items to choose from: Pacific Rim Platter—pot stickers with seared `ahi, rice, Asian noodle salad and peanut dressing; Cilantro Pesto `Ahi; Macnut encrusted Ono with wasabi cream, and many vegetarian selections. A full espresso bar, scrumptious pastries and desserts make for a perfect afternoon treat. Some of their homemade condiments (Tropical Fruit Chutney, and Guava Jungle Jazz Sauce) are bottled and for sale.

Caffé Coco is open 9 a.m. to 9 p.m. daily, closed on Mondays. Breakfast, lunch and dinner: $4.00–16.00. Located on the mountain side of the street next to Bambulei, behind the lime green store front and across from Kintaro's Restaurant.

LINGUINE WITH `AHI, LEMON, BASIL AND SUNDRIED TOMATO

1 pound `ahi, cut in 1" cubes

½ pound linguine

½ cup sundried tomato, finely chopped

¼ cup extra virgin olive oil

½ cup fresh lemon juice

¼ cup parsley, minced

1 cup green onions, finely chopped

¼ cup fresh basil, chopped

1 Tbsp. lemon rind, minced

1 Tbsp. garlic, minced

½ tsp. black pepper

½ tsp. salt

¼ tsp. hot pepper flakes

For marinade, combine all ingredients (by hand or in a food processor), except `ahi and linguine. Marinate `ahi for 15 minutes while cooking linguine. Place `ahi and marinade in hot frying pan; sauté until fish is just cooked through. Stir in cooked, drained linguine. Serve immediately.

COCO CUSTARD FRENCH TOAST WITH TROPICAL FRUIT SYRUP

1 pound loaf of Hawaiian sweet bread

2 cups heavy cream

5 eggs

1 cup milk

2 tsp. vanilla

Whisk the milk, cream, eggs and vanilla together in a bowl. Lay bread slices in oven-proof dish. Pour whisked cream mixture over bread and soak for 15 minutes or until bread is completely saturated with liquid. Cover with foil and bake at 350 degrees for 20 minutes. Remove foil and bake 20 more minutes or until golden brown and custard is set. Serve garnished with banana slices and syrup.

TROPICAL FRUIT SYRUP (PINEAPPLE, GINGER, LIME SYRUP)

1" cube ginger root, whole

¼ cup fresh lime juice

1½ cups pineapple, finely chopped

1 cup sugar

2 cups water

2 tsp. cornstarch

½ cup cold water

Combine ginger, lime juice, pineapple, sugar and 2 cups of water and gently boil for 20 minutes. Mix cornstarch with cold water and add to syrup, whisking until mixture comes to a boil and thickens slightly. Remove ginger root and serve. Makes about 2 cups.

*W*ho can resist the luscious feeling that comes from the aroma and taste of home baked bread, or warm cookies just out of the oven or a piping hot apple pie? The smells, warmth, flavors and the love that goes into preparing these wonderful soul foods creates a cozy welcome feeling. At Da'Li Deli & Café, everything is homemade; they even roast their own turkey, and creative, imaginative chefs keep the menu fresh with specials inspired by ingredients that are in season.

Owners Dan Seltzer and Elizabeth 'Liz' Foley, who combined portions of their first names to come up with the name for the deli, work long hours energized by the passion and love of their dream. It grew from Dan's desire to have a good New York style bagel on

Kaua'i; he couldn't find one so he started baking them himself. It wasn't long before he combined talents with Liz and remodeled the building Da'Li Deli is now in to a charming and traditional European deli.

They feature an international selection of specials that, as Liz explains, originate from the accent Dan is speaking that day, or maybe a dream one of them had of the Greek Isles, or maybe just a desire for Italy. Their sense of humor and good natured spirits show up on the menu names as well—Da'Li Lama (marinated eggplant, pesto, provolone, tomato and lettuce on foccacia bread) or The Hello Da'Li (fresh roasted turkey, cranberry relish, lettuce and onion on French bread). Both of these sandwiches are superb—fresh and bursting with flavor! They also serve quiches, deli-style sandwiches, salads, and offer their fresh baked breads and a wide variety of bagels for sale.

Breakfast: $3.00–8.50. Lunch: $3.95–6.95. Open daily.

DA'LI DELI & CAFE

(808) 742-8824 • 5492 Koloa Road, Koloa, Kaua'i 96756

HELLO DALI
"fresh turkey sandwich"

turkey breast, sliced
cranberry-apricot relish
lettuce

sweet onion slices
French bread

CRANBERRY-APRICOT RELISH

2 cups dried cranberries
2 cups apricot nectar
½ cup dried apricots
½ cup dry sherry or port

½ cup honey
1 cup water
½ tsp. vanilla

Soak cranberries in apricot nectar until cranberries are plump, approximately 4 to 6 hours. Dice apricots; set aside. Combine sherry, honey, vanilla and water in a saucepan and bring to a boil. Pull from stove and add apricots; let soak for 1 hour. Place soaked cranberries in saucepan and heat; add apricots and liquid; simmer for 5 minutes, stirring occasionally.

BROCCOLI AND CHEDDAR QUICHE

1 pie shell, unbaked
15 eggs
½ cup milk
1 pint sour cream
¾ pound sharp white cheddar cheese
¾ pound sharp yellow cheddar cheese

2 onions
2 bunches of broccoli
4 Tbsp. butter
1 Tbsp. black pepper
1 tsp. white pepper

Preheat oven to 325 degrees. Lightly butter a 10" spring form pan. Next roll out one pie shell until it is large enough to fill the spring form pan. Gently lift the pie shell and line the inside of the spring form pan all the way up on all sides. (This may take a few tries to get the feel for it.) Set aside.

Whisk together the eggs, milk, and sour cream in a large bowl. Grate both cheeses and stir into the egg mixture. Set aside. Chop the onions and broccoli. Sauté the onions in the butter in a large sauce pan until translucent. Add both peppers and the broccoli to the onions and continue to cook for just a few minutes, stirring once or twice to lightly cook the broccoli. Add the broccoli mixture to the egg mixture and stir until evenly mixed. Pour the mixture into the prepared spring form pan, filling until about ½" from the top. Bake for approximately 1 hour and 15 minutes or until the filling is no longer runny. Let cool at least ½ hour before removing from the pan.

*A*ward-winning **Dondero's** features fine regional Italian cuisine in an elegant atmosphere. The restaurant's interior is graced with an inlaid marble floor, magnificent Franciscan murals and 2500 hand-painted seashells that decorate the walls; you are sure to feel like royalty. If you'd like to enjoy dining outside in the balmy tropical night air surrounded by beautiful gardens, Dondero's offers a lovely piazza where the ambiance is enhanced by the sound of the ocean waves.

Utilizing fresh local ingredients, the chefs at Dondero's create many delicious items to choose from: Grilled Portabella Mushroom Salad, Pesce Fresco (Hawaii's Fresh Fish special of the day), Spaghettini Alla Pescatora (fisherman's pasta with clams, mussels, fresh fish, scallops, shrimp and crab in a rich tomato and lobster sauce.) Wow! Or, try this tantalizing combination: Veal Scaloppini with Lobster—tender veal gently sautéed with fire-roasted sweet peppers, asparagus and spinach, topped with steamed Lobster and Marsala demi-glace. If you're not too full after all of this, indulge in their Tiramisu or Chocolate-Chocolate Torte and choose from an appealing selection of after dinner drinks.

Please call for reservations. Nice resort wear required (no thongs or T-shirts). Dinner nightly. Entrées: $16.50–28.00.

CARPACCIO

2½ oz. beef tenderloin, thinly sliced

2 oz. mixed greens

½ oz. pesto with mayonnaise
(pesto 1 part, mayo 2 parts)

½ oz. horseradish with mayonnaise
(horseradish 1 part, mayo 2 parts)

½ oz. balsamic dressing

½ oz. extra virgin olive oil

pinch cracked black pepper

1 taro or other type bread stick dough

Hawaiian salt

Put thinly sliced filet on cold plate, completely covering the bottom, but not touching the rim. Decorate the carpaccio with the sauces from squeeze bottles. Mix tossed greens with balsamic vinegar. Place in center of beef.

Preheat oven to 350 degrees. Roll out 1 piece of the taro roll dough that has been cut in ¼" slices and start making bread sticks. Brush with water; then sprinkle with salt. Bake for 3–5 minutes until golden brown. Sprinkle with cracked pepper when done.

PORCINI CREPES
CREPES

7 oz. flour

2 oz. butter

1 cup milk

6 eggs

1 cup cream

salt and pepper to taste

Combine flour and melted butter; then add milk, eggs and cream. Pass the mixture through a sieve. Heat sauté pan, using oil or non-stick spray to make crepes.

PORCINI STUFFING

1½ oz. Porcini mushrooms, sliced

5 oz. mushrooms, sliced

1 Tbsp. chopped garlic

1 cup white wine

4 oz. butter

1 cup flour

1 cup cream

1 cup fontina cheese

½ cup parmesan cheese

Cook Porcini with domestic mushrooms, garlic and white wine; reduce. Take out of pan and add butter and flour. Cook until nutty smelling; then add cream and thicken. Add mushrooms again. Combine fontina and parmesan cheese into mixture to make stuffing. Put into crepes. Fold crepes 2 times to make a triangle. Garnish with Parmesan Cream Sauce and lightly sprinkle with parmesan cheese.

PARMESAN CHEESE CREAM SAUCE

½ Tbsp. chopped garlic

olive oil

1 cup heavy cream

2 oz. fresh parmesan cheese

Sauté garlic in olive oil until tender. Add heavy cream; simmer and reduce by half (should have a creamy texture). Add parmesan cheese.

Executive Chef David W. Boucher

*L*ovely and gracious are two words that come to mind when thinking of **Gaylord's Restaurant**, which is set in a charming courtyard offering a quiet elegance. Beautiful gardens and a view of Kauai's lush green hills leading to Mt. Wai`ale`ale (the rainiest spot on earth) enhance the warm welcoming atmosphere of the 16,000 square foot historic plantation owner's home where Gaylord's is located. Horse drawn carriage rides are available for tours of the 35-acre estate that surrounds the home, which was built in 1935 and also houses small boutiques.

In 1986, Wally and Roberta Wallace moved to Kaua`i from Alaska because they "couldn't resist the challenge of creating a restaurant from scratch." Well, it's obvious that they have been successful in their endeavor. Gaylord's is considered one of Hawai`i's most romantic restaurants; they have been featured in *Gourmet Magazine* and they received the Hale `Aina Restaurant-of-Distinction Award 2000.

Gaylord's welcomes families and also hosts special occasions: parties, weddings and receptions. A couple nights a week, Gaylord's presents a Lu`au on the grounds (not at the restaurant) featuring quality food and a dynamic, fast-paced show suitable for the whole family. Call for nights the Lu`au is featured.

Seafood Rhapsody is a long-standing dinner favorite: grilled jumbo tiger prawns, half a lobster tail, sea scallops and fresh catch of the day. Other favorites include Blackened Shutome with Papaya Basil Butter Sauce, and the Hot Crab and Artichoke Heart Dip. A very extensive wine list offers many fine choices by the glass. For dessert, try Homemade Banana Cream Pie and a cappucino. Reservations recommended. Open daily. Lunch: $7.95–11.95. Dinner: $16.95–29.95. Sunday Brunch: $8.95–16.95. Located just Southwest of Lihu`e on the main highway.

GAYLORD'S CRAB & ARTICHOKE HEART DIP

1 pound crab meat (canned is okay), flake the meat

1 quart mayonnaise

½ pound canned artichoke hearts, drained and chopped

½ pound mozzarella cheese, grated

salt and pepper to taste

dash of cayenne pepper

dash of garlic salt

juice of 1 lemon

Blend all together. Bake in shallow baking dish at 350 degrees for 30 minutes. Serve with focaccia bread or crackers.

Serves 20.

GAYLORD'S PASSION FRUIT PARFAIT

Mousse ingredients:

6 egg yolks

2 whole eggs

1 cup passion fruit purée, sweetened

1 cup sugar

juice of 2 limes

2 inches fresh ginger, peeled

2 cups heavy whipping cream

For the fruit:

1 large pineapple

2 firm, ripe papayas

Garnish: toasted, sweetened coconut

Flatten the ginger with the flat side of a Chinese cleaver or a heavy sauté pan. Put the ginger, along with the rest of the mousse ingredients, minus the cream, in a stainless steel bowl. Whisk the mixture in the bowl over a bain marie of steaming water until it thickens to a consistency of thick molasses and reaches 160 degrees. Take care not to scramble the egg mixture. Watch it closely and whisk continuously, not to froth, but just to keep it from over cooking and lumping. When the proper consistency has been reached, remove the ginger and place the bowl over a bowl of ice water and stir until it cools. Whip the cream to a stiff peak and carefully fold into the cooled egg mixture.

Peel and core the pineapple; chop into half-inch cubes and set in a colander to drain. Peel and slice the papayas in half. Remove seeds and chop into half-inch cubes. Gently mix the two fruits together and spoon half of the mixture into the bottom of each wine glass. Pipe or spoon half of the mousse over the fruit; add the rest of the fruit, then the remaining mousse. Cover the glasses with plastic wrap and chill. To serve: garnish with toasted, sweetened shredded coconut.

Makes 8–10 servings.

The Hanalei Gourmet is situated in the Old Hanalei School building that is in the center of town. The old school house was almost destroyed by a bulldozer when Gaylord Wilcox stepped in to save it. After paying only $1.00 and signing an agreement to have it restored to its original form, he moved it in 7 pieces to its present location.

With live rock and roll or jazz music on most evenings and a sports bar atmosphere (with a happy hour) in the afternoon, The Hanalei Gourmet is a busy place to hang out and have fun. It is also open for breakfast, offering homemade muffins, Danish, and a few heartier breakfast items. If you're on your way to hike the Na Pali Coast or paddle up a river or just enjoy a day at the beach, stop by and fill up one of their insulated backpacks or coolers with sandwiches, delectable pastries (by Suzi of Suzi's Date Bar) and drinks.

Owner Tim Kerlin (known as Big Tim) is proud of the talented chefs who invent creative daily specials with an international flair. Popular menu items include: Roasted Eggplant Sandwich served on foccacia bread (It's great!), Waioli Salad–chilled, grilled veggies (artichoke hearts, red bell peppers, etc.), Sonoma goat cheese and chef's mango vinaigrette. *Bon Appétit* requested the recipe for the mango vinaigrette, but Big Tim's not telling. The burgers are made with fresh—not frozen—beef. Dinners feature a fresh catch of the day, or Grilled Salmon with a wine dill sauce served with a crab cake with fresh pineapple aioli sauce. Yum!

Open daily for breakfast, lunch and dinner: under $10.00. Dinners: $9.50-18.95.

`AHI PROVENCAL

4 `ahi fillets, 6 oz. each	fresh cracked black pepper
Hawaiian salt	4 sprigs of thyme for garnish

Prepare Tomato Coulis, Pineapple Vinaigrette and salad. Season the `ahi with Hawaiian rock salt and fresh black pepper. Grill to medium rare. Toss the salad with vinaigrette, adding croutons last. Place a fourth of the salad in the center of a plate. Place the `ahi on top of the salad and circle around the salad with about 4 oz. of coulis and garnish with a sprig of thyme. Serves 4.

TOMATO COULIS

1 oz. olive oil	10 oz. diced seeded tomato
2 oz. onion, diced	4 oz. vegetable stock
½ oz. minced garlic	1 Tbsp. fresh basil
2 oz. tomato paste	1 Tbsp. fresh thyme
4 oz. red wine	salt and pepper to taste

Sweat the onions in the olive oil until transparent. Add the garlic and cook until the aroma is apparent. Next, add the tomato paste and cook lightly; then deglaze with wine and reduce by half. Add the tomato and vegetable stock, simmer for half an hour. Add the herbs and season with salt and pepper. Simmer for an additional 15 minutes.

PINEAPPLE VINAIGRETTE

2 oz. pineapple juice	½ Tbsp. chopped cilantro
1 oz. diced shallots	½ Tbsp. thinly sliced green onion
2 tsp. minced garlic	brown sugar, salt and pepper to taste
2 tsp. minced ginger	

Combine all ingredients except oil, sugar, salt and pepper. Slowly whisk in the oil. Season to taste with salt, pepper and brown sugar.

SALAD

12 oz. organic greens	1 oz. sliced olives
4 oz. sliced Maui onions	2 oz. sliced mushrooms cremini
(or other sweet onion)	2 mashed anchovy fillets (optional)
4 cloves garlic, thinly sliced	40 croutons
2 oz. tomato concasse	

Chef Joe Caulfield

or over 15 years, The House of Seafood has been pleasing customers with sensational seafood and gracious table-side service. In a relaxed atmosphere with classic elegant touches, you sit surrounded by greenery with plants inside and a second-story view into the trees outside.

The servers like to have fun, are knowledgeable and encourage questions about the menu and the 10 different fresh fish selections featured nightly, including the following preparations: sautéed, grilled, braised, steamed, broiled, baked, and baked in parchment paper. Along with preparing fresh Caesar Salads right at your table, the servers also provide entertainment when they dramatically prepare a flaming fish entrée or a Flambé dessert. With 80 choices on the all-American wine list, you are sure to find the right accompaniment for your dinner. And do save room for dessert: Haupia (coconut) in Puff Pastry, Mascarpone Cheesecake, Baked Papaya, 2 Flambé specials nightly (Bananas Foster and Chocolate Lover's Delight!). A special Mai Tai and Pupu (appetizer) Platter is featured at a great price from 3 to 5 p.m. Dinner nightly: $20.50–43.50. Children's menu: $7.00–13.00. Reservations recommended.

MAHIMAHI WITH PISTACHIOS AND BOK CHOY

2 lbs. mahimahi fillet, cut into four pieces
¼ cup flour
1 tsp. garlic, minced
1 tsp. shallots, minced
8 Tbsp. butter

8 oz. bok choy torn into 1" pieces
½ cup roasted pistachio nuts, diced small
½ cup shiitake mushrooms, sliced
¼ cup dry vermouth (or dry white wine)

Lightly flour fish and sauté with garlic and shallots in 4 tablespoons of butter for about 2 minutes on each side. When done, remove to serving dish, cover and keep warm, reserving sauce. Heat remaining butter over medium-high heat adding reserved sauce. Add bok choy and cook until it starts to wilt. Add vermouth and shiitake mushrooms; stir to coat leaves and add pistachios. Bring to high heat. Pour over fish and serve.

MO`A KALIMA
(COOKED CREAM)

3 envelopes gelatin
3½ cups milk
1 cup heavy cream
½ cup sugar
1 tsp. vanilla

½ cup macadamia nuts, diced
½ cup roasted shredded coconut
1½ cups fresh blueberries or raspberries
reserve some for garnish

Soften gelatin in ½ tablespoon warm water, then heat in microwave on high for 10 seconds. Heat together: milk, cream and sugar, (do not boil) until sugar is dissolved. Cool to lukewarm and add gelatin and vanilla; stir well. Pour into 4 wide shallow bowls and refrigerate to mold until almost set; then add fruit. When ready to serve, run a knife around the edges to loosen. Sprinkle mixed macadamia nuts and coconut on top. Cover with the serving plate and invert. Garnish and serve.

A welcoming place for the whole family, **Ilima Terrace** offers a beautiful open-air setting next to a lagoon with koi swimming by, graceful swans and a waterfall. Tropical gardens and palm trees lead your eye out to the gorgeous Pacific blue with crashing waves at Keoneloa Bay.

Ilima Terrace features sumptuous buffets that tempt, tantalize and keep you coming back for more. The breakfast buffet is $18.50, and the Sunday Champagne Brunch buffet $28.95, which includes a sushi bar and a shrimp and crab station. Each evening, a theme buffet is offered, and for $28.95, you can enjoy Hawaiian Seafood selections on one night, Italian on another, then Prime Rib night. Items from the Ilima menu include: Sesame Shrimp Seafood Salad, Eggplant Parmesan Pizza and a Pizza of the day, Waimea Prawn Noodles, and a daily fresh fish special. One of the several decadent desserts is the Chocolate "To Da Max"–chocolate ice cream sundae with a fudge brownie, white chocolate chunks and chocolate sauce. Wine, tropical drinks and an espresso or cappuccino are offered to complement your meal. Breakfast: $4.00–18.50. Lunch: $6.00–16.00. Ala carte dinner items: $6.00–11.50. Open daily.

ILIMA TERRACE

(808) 742-1234 ext 4242 • Hyatt Regency Kaua`i, Po`ipu, Kaua`i 96756

RED HOT CHICKEN SPAGHETTI

5 oz. chicken (6 pieces), cooked

6 oz. cooked spaghetti

10 red chilies

½ oz. garlic, minced

½ oz. peanuts

¼ oz. green onions, chopped

6 oz. Kung Pau sauce

salt and pepper to taste

4 scallion flowers

carrot curls

Add to hot pan, chilies and oil and sauté until they "pop." Add garlic and fry. Add nuts, add sauce and toss. Add pasta and toss. Garnish with scallion flowers and carrot curls.

KUNG PAU SAUCE

1 oz. ginger, minced

2½ oz. garlic, minced

1 Tbsp. oil

6 oz. sherry

2 oz. sugar

1 qt. water

2 oz. soy sauce

1 oz. sesame oil

2 oz. oyster sauce

2 oz. sweet soy

1 oz. cornstarch slurry

In large sauce pot, sauté ginger and garlic until soft. Add sherry, reduce by ⅓. Dissolve sugar and add remaining ingredients. Thicken with cornstarch slurry until consistency of maple syrup. Keep in pour container for use.

WAIMEA PRAWN NOODLES

6 Contessa shrimp, raw

4 oz. noodles

1 oz. oil

1 tsp. garlic, chopped

1 tsp. shallot, chopped

1½ oz. shrimp sambal

2 oz. won bok, julienne

1 oz. baby bok choy, halved (4 pieces)

1 egg

1 oz. mung bean sprouts

1½ oz. sweet soy

2 oz. carrots, julienne

6 pieces shrimp crackers

pinch of fried shallots

pinch of green onions, chopped

Place noodles in pasta pot to cook. Heat wok until hot; add oil and shrimp. Cook until well seared. Add garlic and shallots; cook until slightly browned. Add shrimp sambal; mix thoroughly, cook until sweet. Add bok choy and scramble egg.

Remove noodles from water; drain briefly. Add to wok; fry and toss with other ingredients. Add sweet soy, lightly caramelize. Season with salt and pepper. Garnish with shrimp crackers, fried shallots and green onions.

In the first edition of *Tasting Paradise*, I wrote that Kalaheo Coffee Co. & Café is the kind of place that every neighborhood loves and needs. It is still true, and John and Kristina Ferguson are still serving delicious food, pastries and coffee to neighbors and to visitors passing through on their way to Waimea Canyon and Koke'e State Park. Casual and friendly with great food at reasonable prices, Kalaheo Coffee Co. is a good place to meet a friend for lunch, relax and read a book with a pastry and a cappuccino, choose some tasty picnic items to go, or stock up on Hawaiian and international coffees sold by the pound. John enjoys exploring the different coffee flavors and makes his own house blends as well, so there's a lot to choose from.

They start serving breakfast early with popular items such as Tropical French Toast, Bonzo Burrito Tortilla Wrap and Veggie Tofu Wrap. For lunch, the fresh fish daily special is a treat! Or try the soup of the day with a deli sandwich. Other favorites include Grilled Turkey Burger, the Herb Chicken Breast, and Pasta and Island Greens. The produce is from local Kalaheo farmers. Macadamia Nut Shortbread, Peanut Butter Cookies, homemade Biscotti, Mango Scones (in season), various flavors of coffee cakes and muffins, and their specialty—yummy Cinnamon Knuckles are won-

derful with one of the many featured coffee drinks (or teas). Open daily until 4 p.m., except Sundays, until 2 p.m. Breakfast: $2.95–6.75. Lunch: $4.75–8.95. Find Kalaheo Coffee Co. & Café on the internet at kalaheo.com.

KALAHEO COFFEE CO. & CAFE

(808) 332-5858 • 2–2436 Kaumualii Highway, Kalaheo, Kaua'i 96741

CHEESECAKE

2 pounds softened cream cheese

1 cup sugar

2 tsp. vanilla

4 eggs at room temperature

1 oz. flavoring syrup (mango syrup or any coffee flavoring syrup)

1 cup fresh diced mango, or fruit of choice

In table top mixer with paddle, cream sugar, cream cheese and vanilla until smooth and fluffy. Scrape down bowl twice and whip mixture until light. Fold in one egg at a time and whip until light and fluffy. Fold in syrup and fruit.

CRUST

10.5 oz. graham cracker or ginger snap crumbs

4 oz. melted butter

2 tsp. cinnamon

Mix all ingredients together and press with fingers into removable bottom pan, coating pan evenly.

Pour cheesecake mixture into crust and bake at 300 degrees for 40 minutes until firm. With cheesecake still in oven, turn oven off and set timer for another 40 minutes. Cool on rack until room temperature. Place into refrigerator over night. Freeze the following day.

CHOCOLATE MAC NUT BISCOTTI

½ pound butter

1½ cups sugar

4 eggs

8 tsp. syrup flavoring

2 tsp. vanilla

4 cups flour

3 tsp. baking powder

½ tsp. salt

1 cup macadamia nuts, chopped (or other type of nuts)

1 cup semi sweet chocolate, chopped

Cream butter and sugar until fluffy. Add eggs one at a time and beat until fluffy again. Mix in the syrup and vanilla. Sift flour, baking powder and salt together and mix into the creamed mixture. Stir in the nuts and chopped chocolate. Divide dough into two loaves. Freeze until firm. Bake at 325 degrees for 20 minutes.

Let cool to be able to handle and slice; then place on pan. Bake each side for 10 minutes at 300 degrees to dry out the biscotti. Coat with melted chocolate; and garnish with chopped macadamia nuts.

(The dough may be divided into 3 or 4 loaves and frozen until ready to bake. Make sure they are wrapped tightly with plastic wrap and place into freezer baggie.)

On the way up to Koke`e State Park, you will pass by one of the many awe-inspiring sights on Kaua`i—Waimea Canyon, which is known as the Grand Canyon of the Pacific. A bit farther up the road (at about 3,600 feet elevation), you'll notice the air getting considerably cooler and you'll enter beautiful Koke`e State Park where there are forests, many hiking trails and a terrain that most would not think of finding in Hawai`i.

Past the lodge and at the end of the road, there are two viewing points showing off the breathtakingly beautiful primordial Kalalau Valley and blue Pacific. The view is

often obscured by chilly clouds blowing through the area. If you are patient (bring warm clothes), you will be rewarded. Remember the Koke`e Lodge is there to warm you up with a bowl of their popular Portuguese Bean Soup ("local soul food") and chili. They also have sandwiches, fresh vegetarian selections, some unique and flavorful salads: Moroccan Salad, Blue Cheese and Pear Salad, Greek Salad. For dessert, try homemade Lilikoi or Shredded Coconut Pie, or Carrot Cake with some Kaua`i grown French roast coffee. Cocktails, Kaua`i brewed beers, and wine are served as well.

The gift shop features many Hawaiian made food products with a lot of mini sizes (great for tasting and travel). Examples: macadamia honey, tropical fruit jams, spicy hot sauces, and papaya or mango BBQ sauce—all are made from Kaua`i grown ingredients. Koke`e Lodge bottles their own Hawaiian Pineapple Mustard that they serve on their sandwiches. Locally grown coffees are available, and they have an excellent selection of books on Kaua`i—flora and fauna, history, lore and legends from Kaua`i writers.

If you want to have more time to hike and explore the area, cabins are available for overnight stays. (Call ahead for reservations).

Light breakfast and lunch daily. Under $10.00.

KOKE`E CORN BREAD

3 eggs

1¼ cups milk

½ pound butter, melted

3 cups Bisquick

1 cup sugar

2½ tsp. baking powder

¼ cup stone-ground corn meal

Whisk together eggs and milk. Combine dry ingredients. Add egg-milk mixture and melted butter. Pour into 9" by 13" pan. Bake at 350 degrees for 30 to 35 minutes.

KOKE`E LODGE "SHREDDED COCONUT PIE"

4 – 9" pie shells, unbaked

12 – 1 oz. squares unsweetened chocolate

18 oz. shredded sweetened coconut

¼ cube butter, melted

1 tsp. salt

1 dozen eggs

4 cups light corn syrup

2 Tbsp. vanilla

Place 3 squares of chocolate in each pie shell, then pre-bake pie shell for 4 minutes at 425 degrees to melt chocolate. Carefully spread the chocolate evenly in the bottom of the shell. Divide coconut evenly into the 4 pie shells. In mixing bowl, add salt, eggs, corn syrup, vanilla and melted butter. Mix 3 minutes. Pour into pie shells and bake at 425 degrees for 15 minutes, then at 375 degrees for 25 minutes.

Caution: Oven temperatures can vary—watch and check during baking time. A toothpick test is recommended.

LA CASCATA

(808) 826-2761 • Princeville Resort, Princeville, Kaua'i 96722

As the sky changes from bright sunset hues reflecting on the ocean into soft glowing twilight, the beautiful Bali Hai view you'll see from La Cascata becomes a silhouette. Try to arrive early for dinner to capture a glimpse of this spectacular setting and see if there are any waterfalls cascading down the mountains. They are the inspiration for La Cascata's name, which means "the cascade." Already, you are in one of the most beautiful and timeless places in the world. Inside La Cascata, this splendor is combined with a feeling of being transported to yet another place and time with columns, arches, muted colors of gold and rose, hand-painted murals of Italian villages and trompe l'oeil ivy gracefully curling along the ceiling and walls.

Discreet and attentive service accompanies artistically presented delicious food. Kaua'i Arugola salad with pears, Gorgonzola cheese and walnut vinaigrette is a great flavorful beginning and can lead into Sautéed Kona Lobster, shrimp, scallops and clams on linguine pasta with a spicy tomato sauce or Grilled Island `Ahi on primavera risotto and saffron tomato cream sauce. I found the dessert presentation to be especially spectacular. Try the Tiramisu and Polenta Poundcake with fresh berries and mascarpone cheese. Luscious! La Cascata also features an extensive wine list.

Dinner nightly. Entrées: $22.95–32.95. Reservations recommended.

INSALATA DI TONNO E PATATE
(TUNA AND POTATO SALAD)

8 small new potatoes

1 pound fresh tuna

1 clove garlic, crushed

2 oz. olive oil

1 medium red onion, sliced thin

3 Tbsp. wine vinegar

¼ cup parsley, chopped

salt and pepper to taste

Boil the potatoes in their skins until tender. Dice the potatoes medium size when still warm. Also while still warm, season with garlic, oil, onions and vinegar, then salt, pepper and parsley. Cut the tuna into strips 2½" square. Rub with olive oil, salt and pepper. Grill over an open flame a few minutes on each side so that the center remains rare. Allow to cool completely; then slice in ¼" slices. Arrange around potato salad.

Serves 4.

FIRE ROASTED RACK OF LAMB
ON SOFT PORCINI MUSHROOM POLENTA

Executive Chef Mark D. Secker

2 racks of lamb, 8 bones each, cleaned
  and Frenched

Fennel Dust Seasoning ingredients:

2 oz. coriander seeds

2 oz. fennel seeds

1 cinnamon stick

1 piece of star anise

pinch of salt

pinch of pepper

1 oz. sugar

Polenta ingredients:

2 oz. olive oil

1 Tbsp. garlic, chopped

⅛ tsp. red chili flakes

2 oz. dried Porcini mushrooms, soaked

4 cups chicken broth

1½ cups corn meal

1 cup heavy cream

¼ cup freshly grated parmesan cheese

¼ pound whole butter

2 Tbsp. Italian parsley, finely chopped

Toast first 4 Fennel Dust Seasoning ingredients in a sauté pan over medium heat. Then add salt, pepper, and sugar and grind in a spice or coffee grinder. Set aside. For Polenta: Heat oil in large heavy-bottomed pot. Add garlic, chili flakes, mushrooms and stock. Bring to a boil and lower to simmer. While simmering, slowly add the corn meal, stirring constantly. Continue to stir with a wire whip and cook for about 15 minutes. Remove from heat and stir in the cream, cheese, butter and parsley.

Season the racks with Fennel Dust Seasoning and grill over open flame until done. Remove from heat and allow to rest for 5 to 7 minutes. Carve into double chops by slicing down between every other bone. Arrange two chops on a 4 ounce serving of polenta and serve with your favorite grilled vegetables or fresh green beans.

Serves 4.

*S*ince opening in 1992, Mema Cuisine has steadily grown in popularity and has received the *Zagat Survey* "Excellence" Award for 1998 and 1999, a "Distinguished Dining" from *Kaua`i Underground Guide*, and has been honored as one of "Ten Best Restaurants Outside of Thailand" by *Thai Scene Magazine*.

From a humble beginning as a newspaper boy in Honolulu in 1978, the first year chef/owner William 'Me' Choy arrived from Laos in the United States, he and his wife, Rojana have built two successful restaurants with other ventures on the way. In a lovely setting with linens and orchids gracing the tables, you can enjoy specialties that are made with fresh grown herbs from their garden—Kaffir lime, lemon basil, mint, lemongrass and more. Shrimp Roll appetizers and Fresh Island Papaya salad are a zesty fresh start. For an entrée, try the Garlic with Coconut or the Black Bean Sauce Stir Fry—both offered with a choice of beef, pork, chicken, seafood or veggies. You may also enjoy their fabulous food at their other restaurant, Pattaya Asian Café, which is located in the Po`ipu Shopping Village, and offers covered open-air seating. Both locations feature an extensive menu sure to please. Mema serves lunch Monday through Friday and dinner nightly. $8.95–18.95. Located in the Wailua Center.

PINEAPPLE CURRY

2 Tbsp. oil
2 tsp. red or yellow curry paste
4 cups coconut milk
6 Tbsp. fish sauce
1 tsp. sugar
1 kaffir lime leaf, chopped

10 oz. fresh or canned pineapple, cut into square pieces
1½ – 2 oz. pineapple juice
2 – 3 slices red bell pepper
12 oz. chicken, shrimp or lobster
Chinese long thin rice noodles

Soak rice noodles until soft (1 to 2 hours). Cut to approximately 2" long. Set aside. Sauté curry paste in oil briefly; slowly stir in coconut milk, add fish sauce and sugar then other ingredients, cooking only until done—just a few minutes. Grab a handful of the soft noodles and add to mixture.

PAD THAI

2 – 4 Tbsp. oil
1 egg
6 – 8 oz. chicken or choice of meat
a bit of pickled Thai radish, sliced
2 – 4 oz. rice stick noodles, soaked in warm water until soft, 1 – 2 hours
1½ oz. fish sauce

1½ oz. lemon juice
1 tsp. Thai soy sauce (Golden Mountain)
½ tsp. black soy sauce
1 oz. sugar
handful of bean sprouts
2 pieces fresh chives, chopped 1– 2" long
1½ Tbsp. roasted peanuts, chopped

Heat oil and add egg, stirring immediately. Add chicken (or other meat). Grab a bit of the radish and stir in. Add rest of ingredients except last three. When noodles and chicken are done, mix in bean sprouts, chives and peanuts.

NOTE: Mema cooks by taste. Amounts are approximate and may need adjustments to suit your taste. Experiment and have fun! The hard to find items can be found at Asian food stores or in the Asian section of most supermarkets.

For golf lovers, and even if you're not, **Po`ipu Bay Grill & Bar** is serving up a tasty selection of breakfast and lunch items in a pleasant location. High ceilings with large windows show off the expansive view of the rolling green golf course (near the 18th green for you golf fans), a pond, and mountains. I've heard there's an ocean view near the 16th green for those of you who like to play. Po`ipu Bay Resort Golf Course is ranked as one of the top courses in Hawai`i and the U.S., and is home of the PGA Grand Slam of Golf.

The menu is developed by the executive chef at the Hyatt and is simple and

well chosen. Breakfast begins at 6:30 a.m. with Mango, Berry and Banana Pancakes and Dungeness Crab Hash as favorites. For lunch, the Pupu Platter is great: fresh `ahi sashimi, spicy onion rings, buffalo wings and calamari. The Grilled `Ahi Sandwich is another good choice or you can try a local style plate lunch with traditional fixings.

Open daily. Breakfast: $6.25–8.50 ($17.50–18.50 for a traditional Japanese breakfast). Lunch: $6.50–10.00. Cocktails and pupus (appetizers) are served every afternoon.

Pass the Hyatt entrance and parking lot and make the next right; you'll see the clubhouse where Po`ipu Bay Grill & Bar is located.

CALAMARI

4 oz. marinated calamari rings
2 oz. seasoned flour
2 oz. tossed greens
1 whole wheat tortilla, fried in basket shape

1 oz. tartar sauce
1 oz. Bell Pepper Aioli
2 pieces lemon wedge (cut in 6's)

Heat oil to 375 degrees. Bury a wok strainer in a large 6" pan of the seasoned flour and place the marinated calamari in the center of the strainer. Shake the excess flour from the calamari by lifting and shaking the strainer. After all excess flour has been removed, place the breaded calamari into the hot oil and fry for 1–2 minutes or until the calamari is crisp and light golden brown. After cooking, remove excess oil from the calamari, draining on a pan lined with paper towels. (The fried calamari must be served immediately and cannot be held for any length of time.)

Sprinkle a pinch of seasoning in with the calamari and toss lightly. Set the tossed greens in the center of the 10" plate. Place the fried tortilla basket in the center of the lettuce; fill the basket with the fried calamari. Set 2 – 1oz. ramekins of tartar and Bell Pepper Aioli opposite from each other on the plate rim. Arrange 2 lemon wedges alongside the ramekins. Serve immediately.

CALAMARI MARINADE

1 cup milk

4 eggs

Mix with wire whip until smooth then strain through china cap. Put calamari rings into holding vessel then pour the liquid over until covered. Must marinate fresh every day. Do not keep for more than 2 days.

CALAMARI SEASONED FLOUR

8 oz. white flour
4 oz. cornstarch

4 oz. salt
1 tsp. red paprika powder

Mix ingredients by sifting through flour sifter into 6" deep hotel pan.

BELL PEPPER AIOLI

4 oz. mayonnaise
1 oz. bell pepper pesto
½ oz. roasted garlic cloves

1 Tbsp. balsamic vinegar
½ tsp. Cajun spice
salt to taste

In blender or food processor, add the mayonnaise and the remaining ingredients and blend well until very smooth and pourable. Add a little water if needed. Taste for seasoning. Pass through a china cap strainer. Transfer to a holding container, cover and store in refrigerator. Do not keep for more than 5 days.

Executive Chef David W. Boucher

*S*ushi Blues & Grill brings a new meaning to the "East meets West" concept offering some serious temptations. They've got the blues as if you're in a Chicago blues club where they serve sushi created by a master sushi chef of 35 years.

Opened in June of 1998, Sushi Blues & Grill has been a hit ever since with its hip decor and theme offering something new and different on the North Shore of Kaua`i. Inside, there are photographs of great blues musicians placed among brick, copper and wood elements with a color scheme of muted blues and greens. Outside the huge wide-open windows of the second story location, you can look out over Hanalei town and up at the towering lush mountains laced with waterfalls.

Sushi Blues & Grill has a very cool and lively bar where you can try a Hawaiian Style Martini, choose from a selection of imported and domestic beers, a variety of sake, and tropical drinks. Sushi Blues features live jazz from 8:30 p.m. on Wednesdays and Sundays, and live music with dancing on the weekends. (Call for schedule).

Favorite sushi choices: Las Vegas Roll (hot on the outside, cool on the inside) tuna, yellow tail and avocado in a tempura battered roll, or Crunchy Roll—tempura shrimp, chili sauce and tobiko eggs rolled in tempura flake. Other specialties include Macadamia Nut Shrimp with Thai Chili Plum Sauce and Pacific Scallops in Cilantro Pesto Cream.

Sushi $4.00–17.95 (for a combination platter). Whole dinners $13.95–21.95. Dinner served 6–10 p.m. Closed Mondays.

SUSHI BLUES & GRILL

(808) 826-9701 • Ching Young Village, Hanalei, Kaua`i 96714

FRESH ONO IN GARLIC SAKE CREAM SAUCE

1 – 8 oz. fresh ono fillet or fresh local white fish

4 oz. table grade sake

3 cloves fresh garlic, minced

2 oz. heavy cream

1 oz. fish stock, or clam base as substitute

dash salt and white pepper

½ oz. lemon grass oil, or lemon zest as substitute

dash of minced Chinese parsley

flour for coating

peanut oil for sautéing

Lightly coat fish in flour and sauté in a small amount of peanut oil. Add a dash of the sake while sautéing; remove fish from pan when cooked. In the same pan, add another 2 ounces of sake, with salt, pepper, garlic, lemon grass oil and Chinese parsley. Allow sake to reduce; then add cream, fish stock and the rest of the sake. Allow this to reduce over high heat until sauce thickens. Arrange fish on plate and finish with garlic sake cream sauce.

SHRIMP TEMPURA CRUNCHY ROLL

2 – 16/20 tiger prawns, peeled and deveined

6 cups vegetable oil for deep frying

¼ cup sticky sushi rice (long grain white rice, rice vinegar, sugar)

1 sheet sushi nori*

1 tsp. tobiko (flying fish roe)

tempura batter

½ cup mayonnaise, mixed with:

1 tsp. chili sesame oil

2 tsp. sweet unagi sauce*

Prepare tempura batter per instructions on package. Heat 6 cups vegetable oil in large wok. Batter prawns in tempura and fry in oil until golden brown. Set aside on paper towels to drain and cool. Prepare tempura flakes by drizzling ¼ cup tempura batter directly into hot oil. Batter will bead into individual flakes. Remove with strainer when golden brown. Allow to drain and cool. Prepare rice as follows: rinse rice 3 times then soak in water for 1 hour. After soaking, cook rice in automatic rice cooker. Proportions of rice to water are as follows: 1⅕ cups water to 1 cup dry rice. When finished cooking, empty rice into large bowl (wooden, if possible), stir to cool and mix in 7 tablespoons rice vinegar with 1 tablespoon salt and 5 tablespoons sugar. Allow rice to cool completely before using.

Create the roll by laying out one sheet of nori, wet hands and spread approximately ½ cup sushi rice over nori sheet, spread tobiko over rice, then sprinkle with tempura flake. Turn over so rice is on bottom and lay on a plastic wrapped bamboo sushi roller. Spread 1 teaspoon of chili oil mayonnaise over center of nori, place 2 tempura prawns in center of nori with tails hanging over edges. Roll in sushi roller, cut into six pieces, place on plate side-up and garnish with unagi sauce.

Makes one sushi roll.

*available in the Asian section of most markets

*W*hat a treat to meander through the lush, beautifully landscaped grounds of the Hyatt on your way to Tidepools. As you arrive, you will find grass thatched huts appearing to float over a freshwater lagoon creating a romantic tropical setting. And as the evening sets in, the glow in the sky from the sunset is replaced by the flickering light of tiki torches reflecting across the water.

Tidepools features Contemporary Regional Hawaiian Cuisine. Executive Chef David Boucher explains, "This type of cuisine is indigenous to Kaua`i and Hawai`i. Because of the island's diverse culture, we can use items made from Hawaiian ingredients, such as local somen noodles, local fish, bison, fruits, vegetables, taro chips and even taro ice cream. We are bringing to life the traditional Hawaiian cuisine and presenting it in a new way."

A mouthwatering example of this outstanding cuisine is the Tropical Lobster Salad with mango madness dressing. Tidepools' signature dish is the Macadamia Nut Crusted Mahimahi with a Kahlua, lime, ginger butter sauce and Jasmine rice. Or you may want to try one of the fresh fish specials. Local fishermen call in the catch of the day before the fish arrives so the chefs can begin planning the evening's specials. Desserts include a delicious Warm Apple Tart with ice cream or a decadent White Chocolate Cheesecake with chocolate ganache and blackberry sauce. Enjoy!

Dinner nightly. Entrées: $22.00–34.00. Reservations recommended.

MACADAMIA NUT CRUSTED FISH
WITH KAHLUA LIME AND SWEET GINGER BUTTER SAUCE

2 fresh fish fillets, 4 oz. each

2 oz. macadamia nuts, chopped

2 oz. panko (Japanese bread crumbs)

½ tsp. paprika

salt and pepper to taste

½ cup flour

3 eggs

½ oz. cilantro, chopped

Mix panko, paprika, macadamia nuts, salt and pepper and cilantro in a bowl; set aside.

Take fresh fish, season with salt and pepper and place it in the flour, shake off excess flour, then egg; then bread in the panko mixture.

In sauté pan, place olive oil on medium heat and pan fry fish 2 minutes on each side until golden brown. Finish in oven if necessary.

KAHLUA LIME AND SWEET GINGER BUTTER SAUCE

2 Tbsp. Kahlua liqueur

2 tsp. pickled ginger, minced

1 Tbsp. butter

1 tsp. shallots

1 Tbsp. heavy cream

1 Tbsp. lime juice

In a sauce pan, add Kahlua, lime shallots, ginger and heavy cream. Let it simmer until half of the volume is gone. Turn heat very low. Using a wire whisk, slowly whisk butter a little at a time until you have a smooth sauce.

STEAMED SNAPPER

2 – 3.5 oz. pieces snapper

pinch scallion

½ tsp. ginger

½ tsp. garlic

salt and pepper to taste

1 cup soy sauce

2 Tbsp. sesame oil

2 oz. bok choy

2 oz. snap peas

1 oz. red bell pepper, julienne

2 oz. shiitake mushrooms (quartered)

2 oz. asparagus tips

Mix soy sauce and sesame oil. Sauté bok choy, snap peas, red bell pepper, shiitake mushrooms and asparagus tips in salad oil. Steam fish until tender and top with above mixtures.

Executive Chef David W. Boucher

O`ahu

The Gathering Place

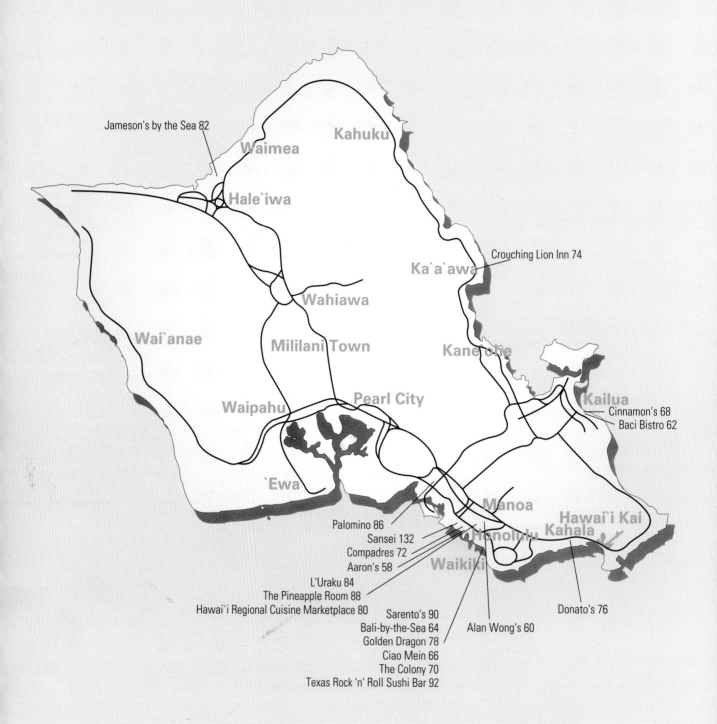

Jameson's by the Sea 82

Waimea

Kahuku

Hale`iwa

Crouching Lion Inn 74

Ka`a`awa

Wahiawa

Wai`anae

Mililani Town

Kane`ohe

Kailua

Pearl City

Cinnamon's 68
Baci Bistro 62

Waipahu

`Ewa

Palomino 86
Sansei 132
Compadres 72
Aaron's 58

Manoa

Hawai`i Kai
Kahala

Honolulu

L'Uraku 84
The Pineapple Room 88
Hawai`i Regional Cuisine Marketplace 80

Waikiki

Sarento's 90
Bali-by-the-Sea 64
Golden Dragon 78
Ciao Mein 66
The Colony 70
Texas Rock 'n' Roll Sushi Bar 92

Donato's 76

Alan Wong's 60

O'ahu

Restaurant, Page, Type of Cuisine,
Recipes Featured

*I*t's an extravagant feeling to be dining on top of the world, well, actually on the 36th floor of the Ala Moana Hotel where Aaron's atop the Ala Moana is located. Formerly the home of Tri–Star Restaurant Group's signature restaurant Nicholas Nickolas, the pristine location received a $1 million makeover and re-opened named in honor of Aaron Placourakis, President and CEO of the successful company. The three partners that make up the Tri–Star Restaurant Group, Jiro Noguchi, Al Souza and Mr. Placourakis share a common philosophy, "Each restaurant is an extension of ourselves. You're coming to our home when you come to dine with us at Tri–Star Restaurants. Everyone is treated like a star."

Keeping the successful elements of the former restaurant—award-winning cuisine, outstanding views and superb service, Aaron's creates an inviting atmosphere with cool ocean colors, jewel-tone glass mosaics and warm cherry wood accents.

With an impressive selection of fine domestic and imported wines available from the restaurant's 2,000 bottle wine cellar, you are sure to find the perfect complement for your dinner.

The Greek Maui Wowie Special salad is a fabulous burst of fresh zesty flavors— Tomatoes, avocado, Maui onions, feta cheese and bay shrimp. Signature dishes include Live Maine Lobster, Opaka Katina with lemon butter and capers; Veal King Oscar with king crab potato cake, asparagus and bernaise. Aaron's also features the "freshest seafood and finest meats." For a dramatic finish, try the fresh Strawberries Panzini, which are flambéed at your table.

Open nightly. Entrées from $18.95. Also, check out Sarento's (page 90) and Nick's Fishmarket Maui (page 124).

SHRIMP CRACKER CRUSTED OPAH
WITH JICAMA SHIITAKE MUSHROOM SLAW

4 opah back fillets, 7 oz. each

½ package shrimp crackers (4.75 oz.)
   Komodo brand

2 oz. butter, clarified

oil for deep frying

Deep fry crackers at 350 degrees until crispy. Remove from oil and place on paper towel to absorb excess oil; then place into food processor with clarified butter. Run processor until crackers become fine crumbs. (If saving for later use, remove and place in labeled air-tight container. Don't refrigerate—it will cause crumbs to harden.)

Sear both sides of fish, then pat crumbs lightly on one side. Place on broiler pan with crumb side up and bake in 350 degree oven until fish is cooked to desired temperature.

To serve: Mix Miso Dressing with slaw vegetables. Place on plate, then place cooked crusted fish on top and drizzle with Cilantro Parsley Oil (recipe below).

JICAMA SHIITAKE MUSHROOM SLAW

1 pound jicama, peeled and julienned fine

1 pound shiitake mushrooms, stem
   removed and sliced thin

¼ pound carrots, peeled and julienned fine

¼ pound red onion, peeled and julienned

½ pound head cabbage, sliced fine

Mix above vegetables together.

Ingredients for Miso Dressing:

1 cup white miso paste

1 lemon, juice and zest

1½ cups mayonnaise

1 tsp. ground coriander

½ tsp. garlic, chopped

1 Tbsp. cilantro, chopped

1½ Tbsp. fresh ginger, peeled and grated

2 Tbsp. red wine vinegar

1 pinch salt and pepper

Mix all together in a bowl with a whisk.

CILANTRO PARSLEY OIL

2 Tbsp. cilantro, chopped

2 Tbsp. Italian parsley, chopped

¾ cup olive oil

1 pinch salt

Place all in a blender and purée. Put in squirt bottle.

ALAN WONG'S RESTAURANT

(808) 949-1939 • 1857 South King Street, Honolulu, O`ahu 96826

*H*is food has been described as innovative, imaginative, and even witty. He is known for his humbleness, sense of humor and creativity. His exceptionally popular restaurant won the Hale `Aina award for "Restaurant of the Year" in 1996, 1997, 1999 and 2000. Alan Wong, chef and owner of Alan Wong's Restaurant has become a star attraction in the culinary world. Raised in Hawai`i, Alan completed the culinary program at Kapiolani Community College then refined his skills by working and studying on the Mainland, including an apprenticeship at Greenbrier and a 3-year stint at the prestigious Lutece restaurant in New York. Returning to Hawai`i, he became the chef at Mauna Lani Bay Hotel. And now, in his own restaurant, Alan combines his classical training, Asian heritage and Island roots creating dishes such as Ginger Crusted Onaga with Miso Sesame Vinaigrette, Nori Wrapped Tempura `Ahi with Asian Slaw and Soy Mustard Sauce, and Hoisin BBQ Baby Back Ribs.

Alan Wong's Restaurant sits on the third floor of an office building and offers a city view from the glassed-in lanai, an exhibition kitchen and award-winning service.

In 1996 Chef Wong was honored with the prestigious James Beard Foundation "Best Pacific-Northwest Chef" award. *Gourmet Magazine's* readers voted Alan Wong's "Top Food" in Hawaii in the October 1999 issue and many other awards—including `Ilima Awards—have been presented to Alan Wong's Restaurant. Chef Wong, who loves to teach, shares his expertise in his own beautiful cookbook, *New Wave Luau*, which features his recipes with photographs and other interesting information.

Open nightly. Entrées: $22.00–30.00. Call for reservations.

GINGER CRUSTED ONAGA WITH MISO VINAIGRETTE

2 pieces 6–7 oz. onaga
¼ cup ginger, finely minced
¼ cup green onion, minced by hand
½ cup peanut oil
sesame oil (a few drops)
salt to taste
2 oz. corn

1 oz. shiitake mushrooms
1 oz. enoki mushrooms
1 Tbsp. butter
10 oz. Miso Sesame Vinaigrette
1 oz. basil oil
1 oz. green onion hairs
4 Tbsp. panko

Place green onions and ginger in non-aluminum bowl with high sides. Season with salt to taste. Put peanut oil in heavy bottom pan and heat until almost smoking. Carefully pour hot oil over green onion/ginger mixture; oil will boil over the sides. Season with sesame oil. Cool. Sear onaga until brown. Apply ginger/onion mixture to surface, sprinkle panko. Bake at 350 degrees approximately 6 minutes or until cooked through. Sauté mushroom and corn in butter. Spoon Miso-Sesame Vinaigrette on plate and position onaga in center of sauce. Drizzle basil oil around onaga and top with green onion hairs. Garnish with sautéed vegetables.

MISO–SESAME VINAIGRETTE

Miso Dressing ingredients:
2 oz. rice vinegar
2 oz. chicken stock
2 oz. miso
1½ oz. sugar
Sesame Dressing ingredients:
4 oz. rice vinegar
2 tsp. Dijon mustard

1 tsp. fresh ginger, peeled and minced
2 egg yolks
1 Tbsp. peanut butter
1 small piece Hawaiian chili, chopped
8 oz. vegetable oil
2 tsp. sesame oil
2 tsp. white sesame seeds, toasted

Mix all miso dressing ingredients together in a bowl. Set aside. For sesame dressing, place rice vinegar, Dijon, ginger, egg yolks, peanut butter and chili in mixing bowl. Mix well. Slowly add vegetable oil in a steady stream while mixing continuously. When all the oil is incorporated, add the sesame oil and sesame seeds.

To make Miso–Sesame Vinaigrette mix 2 parts Sesame to 1 part Miso dressing.

BASIL OIL

2 oz. basil leaves
½ oz. spinach leaves
½ lemon, juice of
1 Tbsp. chili pepper water

½ Tbsp. garlic, minced
2 Tbsp. water
12 oz. olive oil
salt and pepper to taste

Blanch basil and spinach in hot boiling water; then shock in ice water bath. In an upright blender, place all of the above ingredients and purée until oil becomes bright green in color. Do not over blend as you will loose the color. Pass oil through a fine chinois to remove pulp.

*B*aci Bistro was originally the popular Baci Due on Waialae Avenue and when they moved the restaurant to Kailua in May 1997, they changed the name to Baci Bistro to reflect the ambiance of the new environment. Small and intimate, in an atrium setting with palms and orchids combined with Italian music and some fun, friendly, and even flamboyant Italian servers, Baci Bistro not only serves the windward community but also lures loyal customers from Honolulu to make frequent trips over the Pali to Kailua. There is also a charming and cozy lanai where you can dine al fresco under umbrellas and palms.

Long time restaurateurs, Bill Duval, Nicole Pinot and Chef Reza Azeri (who as executive chef, created the menus from the very beginning for the original Baci in Waikiki) have combined talents and created a wonderful little bistro where everything is made fresh to order. Chef Reza makes his own pastas and sauces that are fresh and light and do not use heavy creams or a heavy tomato base. A Baci specialty is the Ravioli del Giorno (Ravioli of the day); examples are: four cheese; and veal, mushroom and spinach. Other entrées include Vitello alla Baci—veal scallopine sautéed with capers, sundried tomatoes, artichoke hearts and wine; Linguine alle Vongole—linguine and fresh clams in a white, red or natural sauce; Gnocchi con Gorgonzola—potato dumplings with gorgonzola, garlic and fresh tomatoes; also a soup of the day, risotto, and a fresh fish selection. Try the creamy fresh-made Tiramisu for dessert.

Lunch Monday through Friday: $5.50–12.95. Dinner nightly. Entrées: $12.95–19.95.

GAMBERETTI MARINATI

5 shrimp, cleaned and cut down the back
   (15–20's work best)
¼ cup extra virgin olive oil
juice from ½ a lime

3 Tbsp. feta cheese, crushed
   (not mushed)
6 mint leaves, chopped
salt and pepper to taste

Grill shrimp for best flavor; if grill is not available, sauté for a minute or two on each side. In a bowl mix the other ingredients. Arrange on individual plates. If for a party, use a platter. Decorate with thin slices of fresh lime.

(Note from Baci Bistro: This is our favorite appetizer. This recipe is for one serving. Multiply ingredients by number of people who will be served. Obviously, if this is a party platter, you could serve 2 or 3 shrimp per person. Bet you can't eat just one!)

CIOCCOLATO DECADENTE

1 pound dark chocolate
⅓ pound butter
½ cup vegetable oil

4 eggs
⅔ cup sugar

Melt chocolate, butter and oil together in double boiler. In large metal bowl, beat together the eggs and sugar. Add chocolate mixture to egg mixture ½ at a time. Go slowly, making sure the batter is smooth and does not curdle. Butter a loaf pan. Line the bottom with parchment paper. Pour mixture into the pan and bake at 350 degrees for 30 to 35 minutes. Let cool; remove from pan and take off parchment paper. Place in freezer for a minimum of 4 hours. This may be made several days ahead of time. If presenting whole, remove from freezer one hour before serving and decorate with whipped cream. If serving by the slice, place slice on chilled plate and again, decorate with whipped cream. If desired, drizzle with a bit of chocolate sauce.

*I*n an alluring and romantic atmosphere, Bali by the Sea will capture your imagination and please your senses. Comfortable chairs, candlelight, orchids and large open windows that invite the soft sound and breeze from the ocean to come in and mingle, blend with a spectacular view of the sunset, palm trees, lit up cruise ships, and waves caressing the sand.

Selected as one of the top 17 restaurants on O`ahu, Bali received the 2000 Hale `Aina award. What amazed and impressed my partner and me, was the combination of beauty, elegance and perfect service that was friendly and gracious and completely unpretentious. Stephen Fuller, the Hilton's chief sommelier, explained that he prefers to be called "the Bali wine guy." His expertise helped tremendously with their extensive wine list; he suggested a wine that we both loved.

With a wealth of worldly experience, Chef Jean Luc masterfully combines French and Asian influences with Island accents. The food is artfully presented and the flavors are outstanding. Beginning with the `Ahi Trio; then Rock Lobster and Mango Salad, and Asparagus soup, everything was exquisite. I tried the fresh fish special—Grilled Onaga, mango salsa, coconut pesto and sautéed jumbo tiger prawns with creamy lobster sauce—a heavenly combination. Other featured fares include: Rack of Lamb crusted with macadamia nuts and herbs; and Grilled Opakapaka with kaffir lime sauce.

Dinner served Monday through Saturday, entrées: $27.50–34.00. Reservations are recommended. Complimentary valet parking at Rainbow Tower.

OPAKAPAKA WITH KAFFIR LIME AND COCONUT BUTTER
OKINAWAN SWEET POTATO MOUSSELINE

4 portions of opakapaka, 7 oz. each
2 Tbsp. butter
salt and pepper to taste
6 Tbsp. panko

2 Tbsp. Chinese parsley, chopped
2 Tbsp. macadamia nuts, chopped
1 tsp. garlic, chopped

Season opakapaka and sauté until almost cooked. Sprinkle with panko mixed with parsley, macadamia nuts and garlic. Finish the cooking process under the broiler of the oven until panko mixture turns a golden brown color.

OKINAWAN SWEET POTATO MOUSSELINE

4 medium Okinawan sweet potatoes
8 Tbsp. heavy cream
2 Tbsp. unsalted butter

salt and pepper to taste
nutmeg to taste

Steam the potatoes until fully cooked; peel them and blend through a food mill. Add cream, butter and season to taste.

KAFFIR LIME COCONUT BUTTER

2 cups fish stock
4 Tbsp. shallots, chopped
½ cup coconut milk
2 Tbsp. kaffir lime leaves
4 Tbsp. heavy cream

1 medium jalapeño pepper
For Garnish:
24 asparagus tips (6 per serving)
24 tear drop tomatoes (6 per serving)
cilantro

Mix first 6 ingredients together; simmer for 20 minutes. Blend, strain and season to taste.

Set the plate with Sweet Potato Mousseline. Place opakapaka on sweet potato. Arrange asparagus tips and tear drop tomatoes on plate and pour Kaffir Lime Coconut Butter around asparagus tips and tomatoes. Garnish with cilantro sprigs.

CIAO MEIN

(808) 932-CIAO • Hyatt Regency Waikiki, 2424 Kalakaua Avenue, Honolulu, O'ahu 96815

*E*clectic, electric and hip are words that describe **Ciao Mein** where both Italian and Chinese cuisines are served with panache. As they like to say, "Finally the end to the eternal argument . . . 'Italian or Chinese?'" This popular restaurant offers the best of both worlds with dynamic creativity. Original art and furnishings, Chinese sculpture centerpieces and table settings placed at an angle set the stage for the fabulous food that is served family style to allow many tasting opportunities.

Szechuan Eggplant is Ciao Mein's award-winning appetizer. For a salad, you may choose either a Chinese salad or a classic Caesar. Popular entrées include Seafood Fun Lasagna: a delicious combination of assorted seafood, boursin cheese, smoked mozzarella, spinach, eggplant, chow fun noodles and marinara sauce; Chinese Roast Duck Canneloni; and another award-winning dish, Petti di Pollo: sautéed breast of chicken on provolone, garlic cheese and prosciutto. For dessert, (drum roll please) the award-winning Tiramisu is the perfect grand finale.

Ciao Mein has been recognized with awards from *Zagat Survey*, Taste of Honolulu, *Honolulu Magazine* and more. Festive and fun, Ciao Mein is a great place for special occasions. Four semi-private rooms are available, each with a different ambiance. Outdoor seating is also available.

Dinner nightly. Entrées: $15.00–35.00. Call for reservations. Smaller portions are available at half price for children under 12.

Located on the third floor, Ewa Tower. Complimentary valet parking.

WALNUT SHRIMP

1 pound 21-25 large shrimp, peeled and
    deveined
1 tsp. cornstarch
pinch salt and sugar
1 oz. salad oil
1 pound walnuts
1 tsp. honey
3 tsp. sugar
½ Tbsp. salad oil

⅓ tsp. garlic, chopped
1 Tbsp. white part of green onions, cut
    into diamond shapes
2 Tbsp. chicken stock
¼ tsp. each salt and sugar
½ tsp. sesame oil
cornstarch and water
oil for deep frying

Mix shrimp with pinch of salt and sugar, 1 teaspoon cornstarch and 1 ounce salad oil. Dip into boiling water for approximately 2 to 3 minutes, strain and pat dry. Boil walnuts for approximately 15 minutes, strain and pat dry. Add honey, 3 teaspoons sugar and toss well. Deep fry until golden brown (3 to 5 minutes). Strain oil and pat dry. In a wok, heat ½ tablespoon salad oil. Add garlic and green onions, chicken stock and ¼ teaspoon each salt and sugar, cook for approximately 1 minute. Add sesame oil and water mixed with cornstarch to thicken. Toss together with deep fried walnuts and shrimp. Serve hot.

TIRAMISU

26 oz. mascarpone cheese*
1 cup sugar
4 egg whites
4 egg yolks
1 box dried lady fingers**

½ cup espresso mixed with
1 oz. sambuca
cocoa powder
chocolate shavings

Whip egg yolks and ½ cup sugar until stiff. Whip egg whites and ½ cup sugar until peaks form. Fold the mascarpone cheese and egg yolks together. Fold in egg whites. Set aside. In a 2x9x13" pan, layer lady fingers and then with a clean brush, dab lady fingers with half of the sambuca mixture. (The sambuca mixture can be adjusted for your own taste.) Layer tiramisu according to picture. Brush second layer of lady fingers with second half of sambuca mixture. Complete layering. Top with cocoa powder, then chocolate shavings. Refrigerate 24 hours before serving to set mixture.

*available at Safeway or Costco **available at R. Field

COCOA & CHOCOLATE SHAVINGS
MASCARPONE CHEESE MIXTURE
SAMBUCA SOAKED LADY FINGERS
MASCARPONE CHEESE MIXTURE
SAMBUCA SOAKED LADY FINGERS

CHINESE/ITALIAN

HONOLULU, O'AHU

*C*innamon's Restaurant has been serving the windward community of O'ahu for 15 years, with many of the warm friendly staff there for 10 years or more. Quaint and homey with a French country decor and lots of plants, this family restaurant offers a comfortable, smoke-free environment where you can enjoy good, hearty food and competent service.

Cinnamon's is well known as a great breakfast and lunch spot and now dinners are being featured, offering co-owner Chef Carsie Green Jr. a perfect opportunity to showcase more of his talent. A sampling of specialties include: Roast Pork with shiitake caper sauce; Shrimp Curry with mango chutney and 6 condiments; Garlic Chicken or Garlic Steak. Popular family favorites are also on the dinner menu, including Meatloaf, Roast Turkey, Pork Chops, Hamburger Steak, and fresh mashed potatoes. A piece of co-owner/baker Cricket Nam's fresh baked Apple Pie ala mode will complete your experience.

The lunch menu offers sandwiches, salads, Portuguese bean soup and corn bread; there are lots of great choices for breakfast, including Eggs Benedict.

Breakfast served 7 a.m. to 2 p.m. daily, $3.00–9.00. Lunch 11 a.m. to 2 p.m. daily, $4.00–9.00. Sunday brunch from 7 a.m. to 2 p.m. $3.00–9.00. Dinner, Tuesday through Saturday 5:30 p.m. to 8:30 p.m., $8.50–20.00. Reservations recommended for parties of 5 or more.

SHIITAKE MUSHROOM & CAPER GLAZE

2 cups beef broth
3 Tbsp. capers
¾ cup shiitake mushrooms
¼ cup diced onion

½ tsp. garlic, chopped
¼ tsp. black pepper
¼ cup half and half

Bring all ingredients to a boil. Simmer for 10 minutes, add half and half. Thicken with cornstarch. Serve over your favorite roast pork or chicken.

FRESH STRAWBERRY PIE

2½ pounds strawberries, rinsed, hulled
½ cup water
1 cup granulated sugar
3 Tbsp. cornstarch

2 Tbsp. butter
1 baked 9" pie shell
whipped cream for topping, if desired

Crush 1 cup strawberries and set aside. Heat water, sugar and cornstarch to boiling. Boil 2 minutes. Add crushed berries and bring to boil again, stirring constantly. Boil for 2 minutes. Add butter and blend well. Cool mixture.

Fill 9" pie shell with remaining whole berries, stem side down. Pour the cooled mixture over berries completely covering all of them. Chill in refrigerator. Serve with sweetened whipped cream, if desired.

*A*n award-winning steak and seafood restaurant, **The Colony** was most recently honored with awards for "Best Seafood" and "Best Main Dish" at the Taste of Honolulu.

The Colony opened in 1976 with the Hyatt and since then has been providing a pleasant environment with comfortable chairs and cozy booths where guests are served by a friendly, good-spirited staff. Old Hawaiian prints framed in Koa wood decorate the walls and soft jazz plays quietly in the background.

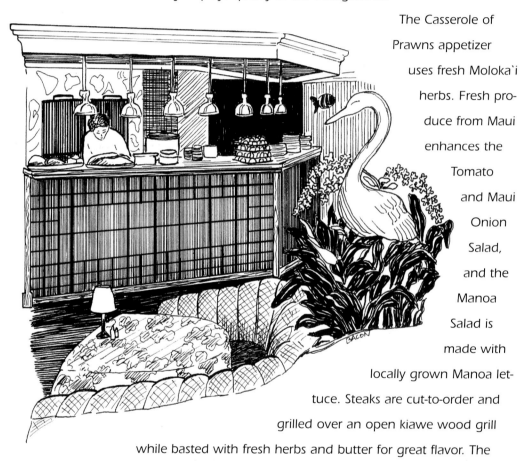

The Casserole of Prawns appetizer uses fresh Molokaʻi herbs. Fresh produce from Maui enhances the Tomato and Maui Onion Salad, and the Manoa Salad is made with locally grown Manoa lettuce. Steaks are cut-to-order and grilled over an open kiawe wood grill while basted with fresh herbs and butter for great flavor. The Colony Hukilau for two—lobster tail, scallops, cockles, prawns and oysters are served in a steamer basket with twin dipping sauces. And what could be better than Chocolate in Paradise for dessert?

Dinner nightly: $19.00–40.00. Smaller portions are available at half price for children under 12.

Located on the second floor of the Diamond Head Tower. Complimentary valet parking available.

NORTHERN PACIFIC SALMON

1 – 10 oz. salmon fillet, or with bone okay
olive oil
fresh basil, chopped

garlic, chopped
salt and pepper

Marinate salmon in olive oil, salt, pepper, basil and garlic overnight. Kiawe wood plank should first be baked or blackened in the oven or over an open fire. Soak darkened kiawe wood plank in a combination of orange juice and Jim Beam's overnight. Spray kiawe wood plank with non-stick spray before putting salmon on. Broil salmon on both sides to make nice grill marks. Place on kiawe wood plank and finish in oven until done. Baking the salmon on top of the kiawe plank will give it a nice smoky and woody flavor.

When serving, place kiawe wood plank and salmon on top of serving platter and garnish with fresh dill and lemon crown. Serve with Lemon Beurre Blanc and Ponzu Sauce.

LEMON BEURRE BLANC

1 cup white wine
2 pieces of shallot, chopped
2 bay leaves
15 whole white peppercorn

1 cup heavy cream
¼ pound butter
½ lemon
pinch of salt and pepper

Combine white wine, shallots, bay leaves and whole peppercorns and reduce by half. Add cream and reduce by half again. Slowly whisk in softened butter a little at a time until incorporated. Add lemon juice, salt and pepper to taste. Strain.

PONZU SAUCE

6 cups shoyu sauce (soy sauce)
1½ cups rice wine vinegar
3 cups water
1 piece dashi konbu, dried kelp 1"x2" size

½ cup hanaktasuo, dried fish flakes
2 limes, juice from
1 lemon, juice from
1 orange, juice from

Combine all ingredients, mix well, cover and refrigerate for up to 2 weeks.

MAUI ONION AND TOMATO SALAD

3 vine ripened red beefsteak tomatoes,
   sliced large
2 yellow tomatoes, quarters
3 oz. red and yellow tear drop tomatoes

1 oz. Maui onion, sliced very thin
1 sprinkle chives, chopped
2 oz. Green Goddess Dressing

Layer slices of beefsteak tomatoes on each other and pour dressing on top. Place the quarters of yellow tomatoes on top of dressing, followed by the sliced Maui onions. Sprinkle the red and yellow tear drop tomatoes and chives around the salad.

GREEN GODDESS DRESSING

2 cups sour cream
4 cups mayonnaise
1 cup olive oil
1 tsp. white pepper
1 Tbsp. salt

1 lemon
½ bunch American parsley
8 cloves garlic
10 pieces green onion, green part only

Remove stems from parsley and discard. Squeeze juice from lemon into blender. Add all ingredients and blend until all items are incorporated.

"*A* compadre is more than a friend . . . With your compadre you experience new adventures in life and relish the memories of adventures past. He is an advisor in the pleasures of living." I like this definition from the Compadres menu—and it continues: "Compadres is more than a Mexican Restaurant and Cantina. It is a place to relax, and indulge the senses with good food, abundant drinks, good company, and friendly service."

A popular spot for its fabulous food and fun atmosphere, Compadres has been the recipient of both Ilima and Hale `Aina awards several times, and even won the Hale `Aina award in three categories for 2000! Compadres offers "Festive Mexican dining and a great place to party!" featuring live music on Friday and Saturday evenings and also for special events, and, of course, a selection of Mexican (and gringo) beers, and award-winning margaritas.

The fresh food is described as, "Western cooking with a Mexican accent." I hear they're becoming famous for their tasty Carnitas. Other taste adventures include Fajitas, Texas or Thai (served with spicy peanut-chili sauce) Quesadillas, Grilled Anaheim Relleno; Fresh Fish Tacos—Aztec spiced or char grilled; and a savory selection of enchiladas, burritos, chimichangas, salads and more. If you've never tried fried ice cream or if you want some again because it's so good, this is your chance!

Founded by Rick Enos and Dick Bradley, the Ward Center Compadres opened in 1984. You can also find Compadres on Maui, at the Lahaina Cannery Mall, and in Northern California.

Open daily. Lunch and dinner: $8.00–19.00.

COMPADRES BAR & GRILL
(808) 591-8307 • 1200 Ala Moana Blvd., Ward Center, Honolulu, O`ahu 96814

OLD PUEBLO SAUTE
(A COMPADRES SOUTHWESTERN ORIGINAL)

1 pound fancy long rice
2 Tbsp. cotton seed oil
1 Tbsp. tomato paste
chicken stock
1 piece chile guajillo, diced
2 cloves garlic, chopped
1 cob fresh roasted corn, kernels from
¼ cup green chile, chopped

¼ cup green onions, chopped
½ cup red onions, chopped
20 prawns, peeled
20 fresh scallops
¼ tsp. Aztec spice (blackened spice)
1 avocado, sliced
Roma tomatoes and cilantro for garnish

Brown rice with oil, mix chicken stock with tomato paste. Pour mixture into browned rice. Bring to a boil. Reduce heat until rice is cooked to perfection. Sauté all other ingredients together. Combine with rice. Garnish with sliced avocados, chopped tomatoes and chopped cilantro.

Serves 4.

CHICKEN TAMAL

1 pound corn masa (corn meal)
3 oz. cotton seed oil
1 cob of fresh corn, kernels from
½ tsp. white pepper
½ tsp. garlic powder
salt to taste
4 dried corn husks

Stuffing ingredients:
3 oz. Monterey jack cheese, shredded
10 oz. roasted chicken, pulled
1 fire roasted red pepper, chopped
1 clove garlic, chopped
4 oz. Ranchera Sauce (see below)

Mix together in mixer: corn masa, oil, corn kernels and seasonings until soft and well blended—for about 30 to 45 minutes. Sauté chicken, red peppers, garlic and Ranchera Sauce together. Soak corn husks in water until tender. Spread corn masa evenly on corn husk; then layer jack cheese followed by a spoonful of chicken, roll and tie each end with string. Steam for about 1 hour until cooked.

Serves 4.

RANCHERA SAUCE

1 onion, sliced
1 green bell pepper, sliced
2 celery sticks, diced
3 serrano peppers, diced
1 oz. cotton seed oil
1 tsp. garlic, chopped
2 Tbsp. castilla peppers, chopped

2 Tbsp. oregano
2 Tbsp. vegetable base
2 bay leaves
26 oz. crushed tomatoes
¼ pound cornstarch
salt to taste

Sauté all together. Bring to a boil and simmer for 45 minutes.

*W*ith verdant steep mountains rising up into the sky on one side of the road and the sparkling turquoise ocean on the other, the drive to Crouching Lion Inn is spectacular. When you arrive at the inn, look for the landmark rock formation in the form of a crouching lion on the hillside. If you'd like to know the legend of the crouching lion, ask at the restaurant. They sometimes have a storyteller sharing legends and spirit tales of Old Hawai'i.

Crouching Lion Inn was originally built as a family residence in 1926, and was converted to a restaurant in 1957. Hawaiian hospitality has been experienced here for many years, and you will definitely feel the spirit of aloha when you are greeted by Frances "Fattie" Bryant, who is the manager and has worked there for over 20 years! Dine indoors or outside on the lanai with ocean breezes and a great view of Kahana Bay. Entrées include: Shrimp Salad, Rotisserie Chicken, Kalua Pork and fresh Island fish purchased daily at local fish auctions. Also, there are hamburgers, sandwiches, salads and their own homemade buns. For dinner, they are known for their Slavonic Steak. Other choices include seafood, steak and vegetarian selections. Desserts are prepared daily in their bakery; the house specialty is Mile High Pie. Try a Polynesian drink to complete your experience.

Be sure to check out the gallery downstairs featuring a beautiful selection of art by well-known artists of Hawai'i.

Open daily. Lunch: $4.95–12.95. Dinner: $11.95–29.95. Early bird dinner from 5 to 7 p.m. nightly (except on holidays) $10.95.

COCONUT ISLAND CHICKEN

⅓ cup toasted coconut

2 Tbsp. butter

1 Tbsp. ginger, finely chopped

1 – 10 oz. chicken breast

¾ tsp. ground ginger

½ cup whip cream

1 large banana

2 large slices of papaya

½ cup coconut milk

lime for garnish

To toast coconut, bake at 300 degrees for 10 minutes; then set aside. In a large frying pan, brown chicken breast in butter. Sprinkle ginger, 1 tablespoon coconut and salt over chicken. Add cream, cover and cook over medium heat for 10 minutes or until done. Remove chicken; put on platter, arrange fruits around chicken. Spoon sauce over chicken and sprinkle with remaining coconut. Garnish with lime.

PEPPERSTEAK

6 oz. tenderloins

3 oz. fresh cracked peppercorns

2 oz. brandy

1 oz. whip cream

2½ oz. brown sauce (demi glaze)

margarine

Slice tenderloins into 2 – 3 ounce medallions. Sauté in sauce pan in margarine until half way done. Remove medallions from pan; charbroil until done. Add peppercorns to pan with brandy and flame. Add whipping cream and demi glaze sauce. Cook until simmered. Pour sauce on dish; top with medallions, then smother with remaining sauce.

"*Y*ou don't need to leave Hawai'i to get a taste of Italy," says Chef Donato Loperfido, co-owner of **Donato's Ristorante e' Carpacceria**, along with his good friend Troy Haley.

It is easy to see the passion, teamwork and love that both Chef Donato and

Troy bring to their creative vision. When their restaurant was just a dream, they traveled to Donato's home town of Alberobello, Italy. Troy explains that while he enjoyed many meals throughout Italy, the best food was with Donato's family. And, in their own restaurant, Troy says they've had guests exclaim, "I haven't tasted food like this since I was in Florence!" And, adding another authentic element, the walls are decorated with artistic wood-burnings of the charming village where Donato grew up.

Carpaccio is raw meat and fish served in appealing and flavorful ways. It is the specialty of Donato's—and as far as they know, Donato's is the only carpacceria in the United States. Chef Donato makes his own sausage, mozzarella, and pasta, and keeps his sauces light and healthy by using wine and oils. Chef Donato's cuisine is based on original family recipes and other traditional Italian recipes. He creates several specials nightly and has mastered the art of making risotto with over 200 different styles. Recommended entrées include: Agnello a Scottadito (grilled lamb chops marinated with fig-flavored balsamic vinegar), Paillard di Vitello (grilled veal scaloppina topped with zesty arugula, fresh mozzarella, vine ripe tomato and gaeta olive salad). And, be sure to sample an exquisite dessert.

Lunch, Tuesday through Saturday, noon to 5 p.m., $6.00–10.00. Dinner nightly: $12.00–28.00. Free valet parking. Italian gourmet specialty items are also available.

OSSOBUCCO CON GREMOLATA

24 oz. (4 pieces) veal hind shanks
1 tsp. garlic, chopped
8 oz. celery, chopped
8 oz. onions, chopped
8 oz. carrots, chopped
1 sprig fresh rosemary
2 sprigs fresh thyme

3 dried bay leaves
4 cups red wine (Barolo preferred)
½ gallon veal stock
2 Tbsp. tomato paste
1 cup demi glace
4 Tbsp. olive oil
salt and pepper to taste

Season veal shanks on both sides with salt and pepper. In a roasting pan, heat olive oil and sear shanks on both sides until golden brown. Remove shanks and sauté vegetables and herbs until golden brown. Place shanks into pan; add wine and simmer until wine evaporates. Add veal stock, tomato paste and demi glace. Simmer on low heat for about 2½ hours. Serve Ossobucco over Saffron Risotto and ladle 2 ounces of sauce over it. Sprinkle with Gremolata and serve.

Makes 4 servings.

GREMOLATA

2 sprigs fresh rosemary
2 sprigs fresh thyme
2 sprigs fresh sage

2 sprigs Italian parsley
zest of 3 lemons
3 cloves garlic

Mince all ingredients very fine.

RISOTTO MILANESE
(SAFFRON RISOTTO)

1 pound Arborio rice
¼ cup white wine
6 oz. butter
3 oz. onions, chopped

8 cups chicken stock
1 tsp. saffron
8 oz. parmesan cheese, grated
salt to taste

Melt 4 ounces of butter in a large heavy pan. Add the onions and cook until translucent. Pour in the wine and reduce over high heat. Stir in the rice and sauté gently for a few minutes. Lower the heat and mix well, making sure that the rice grains are coated with the onions and butter. Add 1 cup of stock, preferably homemade. Add the saffron, and keep simmering. Add stock a little at a time. Stir the rice frequently as it absorbs the moisture. When the rice is tender, but not mushy or sticky, turn off the heat and add the rest of the butter, stirring gently. This will give the rice added sheen and the correct creamy taste. Sprinkle with parmesan cheese and serve.

The **Golden Dragon** was honored with the Hale `Aina award for Restaurant-of-Distinction 2000, adding to the continual list of awards this superb restaurant has accumulated. Chef Steve Chiang has been in charge of some of the finest Chinese restaurants in the United States, Canada, and Taiwan, where he was raised and began his cooking career. Chef Chiang's signature selection includes many tasty dishes: Chicken Egg Rolls, Crispy Won Tons, Island Pork Char Siu, Hot and Sour Soup, Scallops with Lychees and Asparagus, "Lovers of Lobster and Shrimp," Beef with Snow Peas, Chicken Stir-fried with Eggplant in Garlic Sauce, Duck Fried Rice and Green Tea Ice Cream. ($32.00 per person.) The extensive menu features many other tempting items as well, and some unique desserts: Banana Fritter with Coconut Ice Cream, and Chocolate Orange Won Tons with raspberry sauce.

Inside, Golden Dragon is elaborately decorated creating a sense of place to match the food; dining is also available outside on a large lanai overlooking a peaceful lagoon. Lovely tea ladies will visit your table offering exotic Chinese teas and an intriguing description of each person's Chinese horoscope, which can be extremely entertaining.

Dinner served Tuesday through Sunday. Entrées: $11.00–30.00. Full dinners: $32.00–40.00. Please call for reservations. Complimentary valet parking at the Rainbow Tower.

LOBSTER CURRY WITH HAUPIA

8 oz. lobster tails, chunks
1 oz. green peas
1 oz. carrots
2 oz. potato, cubed
1 oz. round onions
2 Tbsp. cooking oil
1 oz. curry powder

2 oz. coconut milk
1 oz. half and half cream
dash salt and pepper
2 oz. chicken stock
2 Tbsp. cornstarch mixed with
2 Tbsp. chicken stock
1 oz. raisins

Blanch the green peas and carrots in hot boiling water. Drain well and set aside. Deep fry the potato cubes for 2 minutes, until cooked; place on the side. Heat wok and add cooking oil. When hot, reduce heat slightly. Stir fry the onion and lobster tail for 2 minutes until cooked thoroughly. Add curry powder, coconut milk, half and half, and chicken stock; stir fry for 1 minute longer. Stir in cornstarch mixture; add the vegetables and raisins; bring to a boil. Transfer to a serving dish with deep fried Haupia on the side for garnish.

HAUPIA

1½ cups coconut milk
¾ cup water
⅓ cup sugar

7 Tbsp. cornstarch
cooking oil

Heat coconut milk in double boiler. Combine and stir the above ingredients until smooth. Cook and stir the mixture over low heat until it thickens completely. Increase the heat slightly and stir the mixture vigorously to prevent it from burning. When the fat begins to melt, the mixture is done. Remove the mixture from the stove and pour it into a 9x8x2" cake pan; let cool until it is set. Cut the haupia into 2" diamond shaped cubes; dust with cornstarch and deep fry for 2 minutes.

GOLDEN DRAGON BEGGAR'S CHICKEN

2 oz. pork, julienne
3 Tbsp. salad oil
2 oz. ginger, julienne
2 oz. green onion, julienne
1 oz. black mushroom, julienne
2 oz. bamboo shoots, julienne
1 oz. preserved turnip, julienne
3 oz. chicken stock
1 tsp. salt
1 tsp. sugar
1 Tbsp. brandy
1 Tbsp. cornstarch

5 pounds clay
6 oz. water
1 whole chicken
3 Tbsp. sesame seed oil
5 Tbsp. duck soy sauce
3 Tbsp. brandy
1 tsp. salt
1 tsp. sugar
1 tsp. white pepper
1 Tbsp. ginger, chopped fine
5 lotus leaves

Stir fry pork in salad oil. Add other ingredients from ginger through cornstarch. Set aside for stuffing. Mix clay in water until soft. Marinate chicken in sesame oil, duck soy sauce, brandy, salt, sugar, white pepper and ginger for 1 hour. Stuff cooked pork into chicken. Close openings of chicken with bamboo sticks. Cover chicken with lotus leaves and tie with a six foot string. Cover chicken with clay. Place aluminum foil on sheet pan with chicken on top for baking. Bake at 425 degrees for four hours.

A dream come true for Alan Wong (see page 60), the Hawai'i Regional Cuisine Marketplace is an amazing venue that provides everything needed to host a successful dinner party, have a wonderful picnic, a romantic dinner for two, nutritious quick bite or simply enjoy a delicious pastry with an espresso.

In Alan's own words, "The Marketplace showcases the best the islands have to offer, from the richness of the land to the bounty of the ocean. Working directly with more than 50 local farmers, we offer the freshest island fruits and premium products, as well as island-bred meats and fish caught in Hawaiian waters, Hawai'i coffee and chocolate, and much more.

"Then we deliver it all to you in a dynamic, "open air" environment, where you can shop, snack, or watch us as we work, preparing everything from "take-away" meals to freshly baked breads, to fresh cuts of local meats."

The HRC Marketplace uses inviting displays to present the abundant selection of foods that include vine-ripened produce (some of which is rarely available to retail customers), rotisserie chicken, homemade soups, take-away meals with a local flair (Honey Guava Hoisin BBQ Baby Back Ribs with roasted garlic mashed potatoes with bacon), beautiful pastries and desserts, fresh baked breads, housemade haupia or lilikoi sorbet and rootbeer float ice cream, and an inspiring selection of specialty gourmet deli foods including Alan Wong's own bottled flavored oils, Li Hing Mui Chutney, Poha Syrup and much more!

Open Monday through Saturday from 9:30 a.m. to 9 p.m. Sunday from 10 a.m. to 6 p.m. $2.75 (for a half cup of soup) to $17.50 for full course meal (salad/appetizer; entrée and dessert).

CRUST

2 Tbsp. butter, melted
½ cup graham cracker crumbs

¼ cup sugar

Line the bottom and sides of a 6" cake pan with parchment paper. In a bowl, combine the butter, cracker crumbs, and sugar. Press into the bottom of the cake pan. Set aside. Preheat oven to 350 degrees.

CHEESECAKE

¾ cup peeled and cubed Okinawan sweet
   potato or regular sweet potato
¼ cup plus 2 Tbsp. canned unsweetened
   coconut milk
⅛ tsp. minced ginger

½ Tbsp. sugar
12 oz. cream cheese
¾ cup sugar
2 eggs plus 1 egg yolk
1 Tbsp. dark rum

Steam sweet potato for about 15 minutes, or until tender. Meanwhile, in a small saucepan, bring the ¼ cup of coconut milk, ginger, and sugar to a boil. Reduce heat to low; simmer for 10 minutes. Reserve 4 tablespoons of sweet potatoes for the azuki relish. In a bowl, combine remaining potatoes and 3 tablespoons of the coconut milk mixture. Mash until potatoes are smooth. In a mixer fitted with a paddle attachment on low speed, cream the cheese for about 5 minutes, or until smooth. Add the hot sweet potato mixture and sugar and continue beating on low speed, stopping the mixer occasionally to scrape down the sides of the bowl with a rubber spatula. Add eggs and yolk, one at a time, letting the mixture incorporate before each new addition. Mix in rum and 2 tablespoons of coconut milk. Pour batter over the crust in cake pan. Place the cake in a larger baking pan with water until the liquid comes two thirds of the way up the sides of the cake pan. If using a springform pan, place the water pan on bottom oven rack below the cheesecake. Bake for 1 hour. Let cool.

18 sections Ka`u or navel orange for garnish

6 mint sprigs for garnish

To serve, divide the haupia sauce among individual plates. With a knife dipped in hot water, cut the cheesecake into 12 thin slices, wiping the knife after each cut and dipping again. Arrange 2 slices on the sauce on each plate; place one piece at an angle near the center of the plate and the other on its end so the point is in the air and crust end is lying on plate. Fan 3 orange segments to one side of cake and place 2 tablespoons relish between slices. Top the relish with the diced sweet potato and haupia. Garnish with a mint sprig.

HAUPIA AND HAUPIA SAUCE

¾ cup unsweetened coconut milk
¼ cup sugar

2½ Tbsp. arrowroot
½ cup water

Line a small baking pan (4 or 6" sq.) with plastic wrap. In a small saucepan, bring the coconut milk and sugar to a boil. Remove from heat. In a bowl, dissolve the arrowroot in ¼ cup of water and stir into pan. Return mixture to a boil and remove from heat again. Pour ½ of haupia mixture into the prepared pan. Cover, cool, and set in refrigerator. In a saucepan, bring the remaining ¼ cup water to a boil. Add remaining haupia mixture; return to a boil. Remove from heat and cool.

AZUKI BEAN RELISH

1 cup dried azuki beans, soaked in water
   overnight

5 cups water
½ cup sugar

Drain and rinse beans. In a saucepan, boil the beans in the water for 30 minutes, or until just tender. Add sugar and boil for 15 minutes. Drain, place in a bowl, and let cool. Dice the reserved 4 tablespoons of the sweet potato and set aside. Remove the haupia from the refrigerator when it has set, dice, and set aside.

Jameson's is known for spectacular sunset ocean views and is a great place to relax, have a refreshing drink and enjoy good food. The first Jameson's was started by Ed Greene in 1975. Now there are 4 locations: Hale`iwa, Kailua-Kona on the Big Island of Hawai`i, and Kapalua and Kihei on Maui.

Daily specials include lots of fresh seafood and the specialty of the house is Opakapaka poached in white wine, topped with garlic hollandaise sauce (recipe at right). Another popular dinner item is their Baked Stuffed Shrimp, and for lunch—the Jameson's hamburger is a hit. Try the chiffon pies (made on the premises) with tempting flavors such as Kona Coffee and Chocolate Mousse.

When the surf is really cranking on the North Shore of O`ahu, Jameson's in Hale`iwa offers a fabulous view of the action. And, while you're there, check out the beautiful gift shop, Outrigger Trading Company, which features a quality selection of crafts by local artists, and try some delicious creamy fudge from The Fudge Works.

The Hale`iwa location has an open-air pub that serves lunch daily all afternoon and dinner on Monday and Tuesday, $7.00–14.00. For casual fine dining in the evening, an air conditioned dining room upstairs serves dinner Wednesday through Sunday, $16.95–26.95. Call for dinner reservations (808) 637-4336.

Kailua-Kona location: (808) 329-3195, Kihei, Maui (808) 891-8860 and Kapalua, Maui (808) 669-5653.

OPAKAPAKA WITH GARLIC HOLLANDAISE
OR SPICY BLACK BEAN SAUCE

6 oz. opakapaka (Hawaiian pink snapper fillets)

Poach in equal parts white wine, fish stock and water. Serve with Garlic Hollandaise or Spicy Black Bean Sauce.

GARLIC HOLLANDAISE

12 oz. butter

½ Tbsp. garlic, minced

2 egg yolks

Heat butter with garlic, strain and let cool. In a double boiler, heat egg yolks while stirring. Remove from heat and slowly add butter while mixing.

SPICY BLACK BEAN SAUCE

3 cans black beans (6.3 oz. per can)
2 oz. ginger, minced
3 oz. garlic, minced
2 cups chicken stock
¾ cup shoyu (soy sauce)

¾ cup sesame oil
1 Tbsp. Chinese chili sauce
1¼ oz. cornstarch
2 oz. water

Mix all together, heat and thicken.

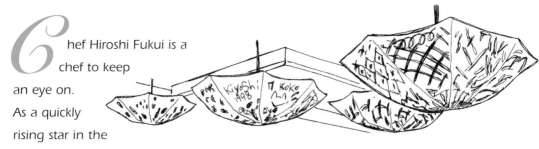

Chef Hiroshi Fukui is a chef to keep an eye on. As a quickly rising star in the culinary field, he is best acclaimed for combining fresh island ingredients with his traditional Japanese training and European influences to create award-winning contemporary cuisine. It seems he is endlessly creative and inspired, something he attributes to the rewarding feeling he receives from his customer's pleasurable responses as well as his constant desire to push himself to the limit. According to him, creativity is a lifelong process and he embraces this challenge with open arms. He enjoys taking basic ingredients and turning them into extraordinary creations.

Like Chef Hiroshi, the restaurant itself is a creative inspiration. Unique and delightful, **L`Uraku** greets you with colorful whimsy—festive umbrellas covered with spontaneous brush strokes by artist Kiyoshi hang upside down from the ceiling. The walls, lamps, ceramics and stools spotlight Kiyoshi's contemporary artwork evoking an air of excitement, fun and festivity as it is the only place in town to dine on award-winning cuisine under a showering of umbrellas.

A sample of L'Uraku's signature Island fish dishes include Papio Fillet, Steamed Whole Moi, Steamed Catch of the Day; and Roasted Garlic Shichimi Crusted Ahi.

As a reflection of L'Uraku's success, they have won the acclaimed Hale `Aina award for 4 consecutive years, including "Best New Restaurant" in 1997 and one of O`ahu's top restaurants in 1999 and 2000.

Open daily. Lunch from $8.95. Dinner from $16.75. Reservations recommended.

SIZZLIN' MOI CARPACCIO

1 whole moi, about 12 oz., filleted
   and skinned

⅛ tsp. salt

⅛ tsp. cracked pepper

1 tsp. garlic, minced

2 Tbsp. soft tofu, finely diced

2 Tbsp. ginger, finely julienned

2 Tbsp. tomato, finely diced, skin only

2 Tbsp. onion chive or green onion
   in ½" lengths

2 tsp. nori kizami, thinly sliced

4 Tbsp. peanut oil

½ tsp. sesame oil

8 Tbsp. prepared ponzu sauce

Slice moi into paper-thin slices and divide among 4 plates, fanning the pieces in a circle. Sprinkle with salt and pepper; brush with garlic. Divide the next 5 ingredients among the plates, layering them as follows: tofu, ginger, tomato, chives. Combine oils in a saucepan and heat until smoking. Pour over fish as it sizzles. Top each serving with nori and drizzle 2 tablespoons of ponzu around each plate.

Serves 4.

MISO–YAKI BUTTERFISH

1 cup miso (1 to 1 ratio of red & white miso
   mixture, do not use sweet white miso)

½ cup mirin

½ cup sake

½ cup water

½ cup sugar

6 – 4 oz. butterfish fillets

In a mixing bowl, mix the miso marinade until sugar has dissolved. Place the butterfish fillet in the marinade for 24 hours. Take the fish out of the marinade and wipe off the excess miso. You can either sauté, grill or bake the fish. But, the best way to enjoy the fish is to grill over the hibachi. This marinade is also good for fish such as salmon, opah belly—fish with some oily texture. Try it with chicken too.

PALOMINO EURO BISTRO

(808) 528-2400 • 66 Queen Street, Honolulu, O'ahu 96813

The first time I walked into Palomino Euro Bistro, I was awed by the interior architecture and design. Representing neo-classic and contemporary styles, it sparkles and curves with high ceilings and stunning hand-blown glass chandeliers, large columns, rich woods and a variety of marble imported from Spain, Italy and Portugal. Palomino is a high-energy urban bistro that is a hot spot for night life, a popular business lunch meeting place, and has been recognized by *Gourmet Magazine's* reader poll for "unerring service," "cooking with originality" and "great fish."

Gourmet Magazine readers voted Palomino "Top for Business" 1999. *Honolulu Magazine's* Hale `Aina awards honored Palomino in 2000 and 1999 as one of Oahu's best restaurants, also in 1999 "Best New Restaurant" on Oahu, and a Restaurant of Distinction "Best Bar" award.

Palomino specializes in Mediterranean and Hawaiian-inspired cuisine utilizing the restaurant's kiawe wood-burning oven and wood-fired rotisserie. Executive Chef Fred DeAngelo has lived in Hawai'i for more than 20 years and is passionate about using fresh, local ingredients. He even creates a special menu with a focus on dishes made with Hawai'i ingredients. Examples include: Paella—saffron rice, chicken, manila clams, fresh island fish, New Zealand green lip mussels, Kaua`i shrimp; Island Ciopinno—Kaua`i shrimp, slipper lobster, scallops, New Zealand mussels, clams and island fish. For dessert—a Molten Chocolate Tower made with Hawaiian vintage chocolate and served with créme anglaise.

Lunch served Monday through Friday, entrées: $5.95–12.95 Open nightly for dinner; entrées: $12.95–28.95. Call for reservations.

PALOMINO ISLAND CIOPINNO

4 – 4 oz. pieces Moi, or other local snapper
8 scallops
8 live mussels
8 live clams
8 Kaua`i shrimp, peeled and deveined

4 Kaua`i shrimp, head on
2 oz. olive oil
8 oz. white wine
40 oz. Ciopinno sauce (recipe below)

In large sauté pan over high heat, add olive oil and sear scallops for 1 minute. Add fish and sauté for another minute; add mussels and clams, deglaze with the white wine, add Ciopinno Sauce, Kaua`i shrimp and bring to a simmer. Cook approximately 2 minutes until the shellfish open and the seafood is just cooked through. Enjoy!

CIOPINNO SAUCE

2½ oz. olive oil
5 oz. Maui onion, julienne
5 oz. red bell pepper, julienne
2 oz. celery, julienne
1 Tbsp. garlic, minced
½ tsp. dried oregano
½ tsp. crushed red peppers

¼ tsp. salt and pepper
1½ cups fish stock or clam juice
½ cup white wine
1½ pounds tomatoes, whole, peeled, in juice, crushed by hand, reserve juice
1 tsp. Italian parsley, chopped

In saucepot, heat olive oil over medium heat. Add onion, peppers, celery; sauté for about 3 minutes to sweat the vegetables. Add garlic, oregano, crushed red peppers; sauté for about 2 minutes, being careful not to burn the garlic. Add fish stock, wine, tomato and parsley. Simmer for about 10 minutes. Reserve. Can be made a day ahead. Hold refrigerated until needed.

FRESH FRUIT WITH SWEET GINGER ZABAGLIONE

4 oz. fresh raspberries
4 oz. fresh blackberries
4 oz. fresh strawberries, stem removed, cut in quarters
4 oz. fresh blueberries
4 oz. mango or papaya, peeled, seeded and diced in ¼" pieces
4 oz. honeydew, peeled, seeded and diced in ¼" pieces

4 oz. cantaloupe, peeled, seeded and diced in ¼" pieces
fresh mint (optional garnish)
3 oz. pasteurized egg yolks or 6 fresh egg yolks
2 oz. granulated sugar
2 oz. champagne
¼ tsp. fresh ginger, peeled and minced

For Zabaglione, combine egg yolks, sugar, champagne and ginger in a stainless steel mixing bowl and whip constantly over a double boiler until mixture thickens and becomes light and fluffy. Be careful not to get the mixture too hot or it will scramble. Once the zabaglione is thick, transfer to an ice bath and cool. Store refrigerated.

To serve: Fill individual bowls with 1 ounce of each fresh fruit, top with zabaglione and mint. You can use any type of fresh fruit available seasonally.

*W*hile the popular Alan Wong's Restaurant (see page 60) is only open for dinner, now similar flavors and quality of dining can be enjoyed for breakfast, lunch and evening appetizers at The Pineapple Room. Located on the third floor of the Ala Moana Liberty House, The Pineapple Room is another Alan Wong venture that opened in the fall of 1999, along with the Hawai'i Regional Cuisine Marketplace (see page 80) also at Liberty House.

Designed to be reminiscent of old plantation days with muted golds, greens and browns, and lava rock around the pizza oven, The Pineapple Room also has a contemporary feel with hanging lights in fish shapes, a dropped ceiling resembling the shape of a pineapple top and an open kitchen bar where guests may dine while watching the chefs. Over 15 wines by the glass and full bar selections are available and can be enjoyed at the Pineapple Room Bar, which also serves coffee drinks and features tempting pastries.

If you arrive for breakfast, you'll find Thai Inspired "Loco Moco"—poached eggs and shrimp, pork hash patty, lemongrass-chili-garlic-black bean sauce; Biscuits and Gravy with Chinese Roast Duck. Waffles, pancakes and yogurt smoothies are also available. The lunch menu includes: Crab Cakes; Thai Cobb Salad; Kalua Pig "BLT" with half Caesar salad; Seared Mahimahi Sour Dough Sandwich and wood oven pizzas. Evening dining includes a great selection of appetizers: Crispy Fried Salt and Pepper Kaua'i Shrimp; Nori Wrapped Tempura Salmon with tomato ginger relish and wasabi soy sauce (this is fabulous!); pizzas and some chef specials.

Open daily.
Breakfast: $4.00–12.00.
Lunch: $7.50–19.00.
Evening dining: $6.00–25.00.

PINEAPPLE ROOM CRAB CAKES

4 oz. crab cake mix	1½ oz. namasu
8 pieces pineapple crown	2 oz. Caper Mayonnaise
½ cup flour	1 Tbsp. Tomato Ginger Coulis
1 egg	1 tsp. basil oil (see page 61)
1 cup panko	1 pinch dried chives

Scoop crab cake mix into 2 ounce balls. Using flour, egg wash, and panko, bread the crab mixture. Form cakes into balls. Rinse pineapple crowns and dry. Stick pineapple crowns (4 each) into top of balls to resemble little pineapples. Gently deep fry crab cake in medium-high temperature oil until golden brown.

Plating: Place tartar sauce in two pools (1 ounce each) on plate. Drizzle Tomato Ginger Coulis and Basil Oil around tartar sauce. Place hot crab cakes onto tartar sauce and garnish with chopped chives.

CRAB CAKE MIX

1 pound flour	1 Tbsp. fresh chives, chopped
4 oz. celery, diced small	8 oz. shrimp mousse (recipe below)
4 oz. onion, diced small	6 pieces water chestnuts, diced small
1 Tbsp. parsley, chopped	

Sweat celery and onions in frying pan with small amount of salad oil. Set aside to cool. Mix all above ingredients together well. Season with salt and pepper.

CAPER MAYONNAISE

4 cups Best Foods mayonnaise	4 Tbsp. capers, chopped
4 Tbsp. Dijon mustard	2 tsp. dashi

TARTAR SAUCE

1 cup aioli	1 Tbsp. onions, minced
1 Tbsp. capers, chopped	1 Tbsp. parsley, chopped
1 Tbsp. celery, minced	1 hard boiled egg, chopped

Mix all ingredients together well. Season with salt and pepper as desired.
Note: For spicy tartar sauce, substitute chili aioli for plain aioli.

TOMATO–GINGER COULIS

¼ cup olive oil	¾ cup tomato, diced
1 clove garlic, sliced	¼ cup chicken stock
1 (½ inch) piece of ginger, sliced	salt and pepper to taste

Heat olive oil in a sauce pan over medium heat. Add the garlic and ginger; sauté until lightly brown. Add the tomatoes and stock and bring to a boil. Simmer, uncovered, for 20 to 25 minutes, or until the coulis is reduced to about ⅓ cup. Transfer to a blender and purée until smooth. Season with salt and pepper, strain into a bowl, and refrigerate until needed.

SHRIMP MOUSSE

2 Tbsp. unsalted butter	2 egg whites
1½ oz. shallots, chopped	2 cups heavy cream, chilled
2 pounds shrimp meat, raw, chopped & chilled	

In small fry pan over medium-high heat, melt butter and sauté shallots just until translucent; cool. In food processor or robot coupe, purée shrimp meat. Add shallot and egg white. Process until blended. With machine running, slowly add cream until it is fully absorbed by mousse. Do not over whip. Remove and place in a bowl. Add salt and pepper to taste.

eginning with a ride in a glass elevator up to the 29th floor of the Ilikai Hotel, Sarento's beckons with an air of romance, style and spectacular views of Diamond Head, Waikiki Beach and the twinkling lights of the city. Under the leadership of Aaron Placourakis (President and CEO of Tri–Star Restaurant Group), Sarento's has won numerous awards and offers exceptional service in a comfortable, elegant atmosphere. Sarento's is named after Aaron's grandfather who was a "simple, unpretentious family man." At an early age, Aaron learned the elements that create culinary success— "quality food, high caliber service, offered in an atmosphere of warmth and in the spirit of generosity and family."

Enjoy a bottle of fine wine, live piano music and superb regional Italian cuisine. Sarento's is an excellent place to celebrate a special event or relish a romantic dinner. Specialties include: award-winning homemade pastas, Lobster Ravioli, fresh Hawaiian seafood (Opakapaka Italiano sautéed with fresh tomatoes, white wine, garlic and basil), Ossobuco, and Lamb Chops Mediterranean—marinated and grilled served with feta cheese, kalamata olives and onions. Try one of the decadent and delicious Italian desserts made by their pastry chef.

Dinner nightly. Entrées: $17.95–32.95. Call for reservations.

The three partners of Tri–Star Restaurant Group also have two other fine restaurants: Aaron's Atop the Ala Moana (page 58) and Nick's Fishmarket Maui (page 124).

SARENTO'S TOP OF THE "I"
(808) 955-5559 • 1777 Ala Moana Blvd., Ilikai Hotel, Honolulu, O'ahu, 96815

TIGER PRAWN & KING CRAB BOLOGNAISE

20 tiger prawns, peeled and deveined   ½ pound crab meat

Prepare Bolognaise Sauce, Lemon Orzo and Balsamic Syrup. Sauté prawns and crab meat in olive oil.

To serve: In large bowl place hot Lemon Orzo, arrange 5 prawns around the outside rim of the plate on the orzo; then pour Bolognaise Sauce in the center. Place 2 ounces of the crab in the center, then drizzle with Balsamic Syrup and serve.

Serves 4.

BOLOGNAISE SAUCE

½ pound onion
¼ pound carrot
½ pound fennel bulb
1 Tbsp. garlic, chopped
¾ pound zucchini
¼ pound yellow squash
¾ pound eggplant

½ pound cremini mushroom
1 tsp. lemon zest
¼ cup olive oil
1 ½ cups white wine
1 Tbsp. Greek oregano
1 quart Marinara (or your favorite tomato sauce)

Dice all vegetables medium size. In medium sauce pan, heat olive oil, sweat onions, carrots, fennel and garlic for 2 minutes over medium heat, then add other vegetables, white wine, herbs and lemon zest. Simmer and add marinara.

LEMON ORZO

1 – 8 oz. bag orzo
1 ¾ quarts chicken stock
1 ½ Tbsp. olive oil
1 Maui onion, diced small
1 lemon, juice and zest

1 clove garlic, chopped
1 cup white wine
½ cup heavy cream
¼ cup mascarpone cheese
¼ cup reggiano parmesan

Cook orzo in chicken stock until al denté, strain (keep liquid), and cool. In sauce pot with olive oil, sweat onion, lemon zest and juice, garlic; deglaze with white wine. Add heavy cream and pasta liquid and reduce until thick; then whisk in cheeses. When ready to serve, heat pasta and add 2 ladles of lemon cream base and serve.

BALSAMIC SYRUP

16 oz. balsamic vinegar

Reduce in sauce pot over low heat until thick. Cool.

Good ol' Texas honky tonk, BBQ ribs and sushi?! Due to the Hyatt's success with Ciao Mein (see page 66) another eclectic dining venue has arrived: **The Texas Rock 'n' Roll Sushi Bar**. Sushi chefs create traditional sushi with a Western twist that is combined with a menu featuring Texas sized portions (everything's big in Texas) of BBQ Pork Ribs, Smoked Free-Range Chicken and Prime Rib.

In this land of contrasts, red bandanna napkins sit on tables next to chopsticks. Wagon wheels, cactus and cow skulls are positioned across from the sushi bar, and cowboys and cowgirls serve food while Ninja bartenders mix drinks.

Entertainment includes watching the high-spirited, upbeat staff, and you can join in on the fun by wearing an inexpensive but good lookin' cowboy hat of your own (offered for sale there), and watching music videos on the "Texas-sized" 8-foot television screen with a state-of-the-art sound system. This is also one of the few places where you can find nightly live entertainment by local rock 'n roll bands.

The Texas Rock 'n' Roll Sushi Bar has won awards from the "Taste of Honolulu" for "Best Pork Dish" for their Texas Style Ribs and "Best Vegetarian Dish" for their Bonanza Vegetarian Cactus Roll.

Recommended dishes include Down by the Sea Texas Pizza—a flour tortilla with lobster, shrimp, crab and spicy topping; Original Texas Style Ribs, Cattleman's Prime Rib; and for sushi try the Rustler Spicy Tuna Roll or Hawaiian Paniolo Roll—scallops, orange tobiko, furikake, avocado, gobo and mayonnaise. For dessert: Peaches and Dreams, baked Indian River peach cobbler topped with cinnamon ice cream. Yum!

Dinner nightly: $15.00–40.00. Smaller portions are available at half price for children under 12.

Located on the ground floor, Diamond Head Tower. Complimentary valet parking.

SAGE BRUSH SALAD

1 head Manoa (or butter) lettuce

1 oz. jicama, sliced very thin

1 oz. Maui onion (or other sweet onion), sliced very thin

2 oz. Margarita Dressing (see below)

edible flowers for garnish

Arrange lettuce on plate and reassemble to look like a flower. Sprinkle with jicama, onions and edible flowers. Pour dressing on just before serving.

MARGARITA DRESSING

2 cups salad oil

¼ cup vinegar

1 cup margarita mix

¼ cup tequila

1 stalk celery, chopped fine

2 oz. Chinese parsley

1 small bell pepper

½ piece jalepeño pepper

½ tsp. salt

¼ tsp. white pepper

dash Lea & Perrin's Worcestershire sauce

Combine ingredients and blend until smooth.

DOWN BY THE SEA TEXAS PIZZA

1 oz. cooked lobster meat

1 oz. canned crab meat

1 oz. bay shrimp

3 Tbsp. Spicy Mayonnaise Sauce

1 tsp. Vietnamese chili sauce

pinch Italian parsley, chopped (reserve 1 sprig for garnish)

1 – 8" tortilla

Squeeze juice from seafood. Combine lobster, crab and shrimp in a bowl. Add Spicy Mayonnaise to seafood and incorporate. Spread seafood mixture on tortilla evenly and bake in 350 degree oven for 10 to 12 minutes on a baking pan until it becomes brown on top and heated through. Remove and cut into fours. Garnish top with parsley and drizzle with Vietnamese chili sauce. Place a parsley sprig in the middle and serve.

SPICY MAYONNAISE SAUCE

2 cups mayonnaise

2 Tbsp. Usukuchi Shoyu (light soy sauce)

1 Tbsp. Vietnamese chili sauce

Combine all ingredients and mix.

Maui

The Valley Isle

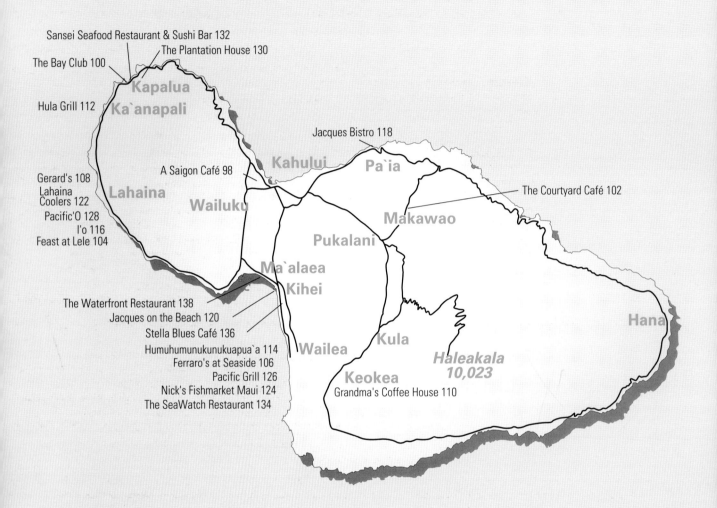

Sansei Seafood Restaurant & Sushi Bar 132

The Plantation House 130

The Bay Club 100

Kapalua

Hula Grill 112

Ka`anapali

Jacques Bistro 118

Kahului

Pa`ia

A Saigon Café 98

The Courtyard Café 102

Gerard's 108

Lahaina
Coolers 122

Lahaina

Wailuku

Makawao

Pacific'O 128

I'o 116

Feast at Lele 104

Pukalani

Ma`alaea

Kihei

The Waterfront Restaurant 138

Jacques on the Beach 120

Kula

Stella Blues Café 136

Humuhumunukunukuapua`a 114

Wailea

Ferraro's at Seaside 106

**Haleakala
10,023**

Pacific Grill 126

Keokea

Nick's Fishmarket Maui 124

Grandma's Coffee House 110

The SeaWatch Restaurant 134

Hana

Maui

Restaurant, Type of Cuisine,
Recipes Featured

*I*magine a restaurant that does not have a sign, is hard to find and has loyal and new customers flocking to it daily. Some who frequent the restaurant do not even know its name. They call it Jennifer's place for the petite, charming, energetic owner Jennifer Nguyen, who confesses she works 8 days a week since opening her popular restaurant in 1995. After becoming bored working at a bank, Jennifer, who thought she'd never go into the restaurant business, found herself taking on the challenge of breathing new life into a dying Vietnamese restaurant. After transforming it into a thriving restaurant, she sold it with the intention of getting out of the restaurant business, only to find herself traveling,

studying vegetarian Vietnamese cooking back home in Vietnam, then coming back to Maui and opening A Saigon Café.

Jennifer says it's easy to be successful. She gives credit to something she learned from her mother—please all the senses. People want to see smiling faces and food that is beautiful, smell delicious aromas, taste wonderful flavors, and hear friendly greetings.

Favorites include: Green Papaya Salad, Hot and Sour Fish Soup, Sautéed Shrimp, and Beef with Garlic & Egg, which became even more popular after Jennifer prepared this yummy recipe on TV. I especially love the refreshing Fresh Shrimp Summer Rolls with Peanut Sauce. Open daily for lunch and dinner. $6.95–19.00.

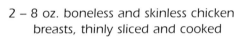

CHICKEN SALAD
WITH SPICY DIPPING SAUCE

2 – 8 oz. boneless and skinless chicken breasts, thinly sliced and cooked

5 cups head cabbage, thinly sliced

1 medium Maui onion, sliced very thin

3–4 large shallots fried in oil until golden brown, drained

2 Tbsp. tamarind paste, dissolved

¼ cup cinnamon basil, minced

¼ cup daikon and carrot for color (optional)

fresh ground black pepper to taste

1–2 Tbsp. roasted peanuts, chopped

Chinese parsley (optional)

In a large mixing bowl, combine all ingredients (except last 2) together and add spicy dipping sauce. Toss well and serve. Garnish with roasted peanuts and Chinese parsley. Makes 6 to 8 servings.

SPICY DIPPING SAUCE

1–2 Hawaiian chili peppers

2–3 garlic cloves

3 Tbsp. sugar

2 Tbsp. fresh lime or lemon juice

3 Tbsp. vinegar

¼ cup coconut juice

¼ cup fish sauce

¼ cup warm water

Combine chili, garlic, sugar in a mortar or heavy bowl. Pound into a fine paste. Add warm water to dissolve the paste. Combine all other ingredients and stir well. This can be garnished with shredded carrots and daikon.

VIETNAMESE

WAILUKU, MAUI

*T*inkling ivories greet you melodically as you enter the **Bay Club** and pass by the grand piano on the way to a romantic candlelight dinner. The sound of the surf and tropical breezes set the tone for an evening of dining pleasure with exquisite food and impeccable service.

In an elegant open-air setting with a view of Moloka'i just across the channel, the feeling of the upscale urban ambiance is juxtaposed with natural island elements. Looking out into the darkness of the ocean at night, waves are lit up by a spot light each time they

explode to a height where they will catch the light and be illuminated.

The sommelier won points with me by offering "the lady" a taste of wine before my partner and I requested it, and he also suggested a wonderful wine that complemented our dinner selections. It pays to ask for a recommendation.

Described by Chef Mark Whitehead as an "Upscale seafood restaurant with emphasis on local ingredients," the Bay Club serves fresh, well-prepared and beautifully presented items such as: award winning Crab and Rock Shrimp Cake, which blend a delicious combination of flavors that burst onto the taste buds; superb lobster; and a daily chef's selection of fresh fish. Fabulous desserts include Chocolate Macadamia Nut Torte and Lilikoi Cheesecake.

Open daily for lunch and dinner. Lunch features a salad bar with seafood, choice of one of 5 entrées and a dessert bar, all for $16.95. Dinner served 5:30 to 9:30. Entrées start at $29.00. Reservations recommended.

SEARED 'AHI TARTARE WITH PICKLED SHIITAKE MUSHROOMS

12 oz. 'ahi tuna
1 Tbsp. sesame oil
2 Tbsp. olive oil
½ cup green onions, minced
¼ cup parsley, chopped
2 Tbsp. capers

1 tsp. chili sambol (Thai chili paste)
sea salt to taste
3 Tbsp. pickled shiitake mushrooms
  (recipe follows)
ogo (optional)

Trim and cut the 'ahi into ¼" cubes. Mix the oils, capers, sambol, parsley and onions together. Season the 'ahi with sea salt. Add the oil mixture to the 'ahi and stir it together. Heat a sauté pan on medium heat on the stove. Add a tablespoon of olive oil to the pan. Place a 3" round mold into the sauté pan. (Mold is to hold the cake together.) Spoon 3 ounces of the 'ahi mixture into the mold and sear until golden brown. Flip the mold over and sear on the opposite side of the tartare. Cook the 'ahi to the desired temperature. Remove the 'ahi from the mold and place in the middle of a plate. Garnish with ogo and pickled mushrooms.

Makes 4 cakes.

PICKLED MUSHROOM SALSA

1 Tbsp. olive oil
1 Tbsp. sesame oil
1 shallot, minced
½ cup green onions, sliced
1 clove of garlic, minced
1 tsp. ginger, minced

1 pound shiitake mushrooms, sliced
1 Tbsp. soy sauce
2 Tbsp. sake
2 Tbsp. rice wine vinegar
1 Tbsp. white wine
1 tsp. sambol

Heat oils in a sauté pan. Add the shallots, garlic and ginger; sauté until tender. Add the shiitake mushrooms and toss in the oil. Deglaze pan with the soy sauce, sake, vinegar, wine and sambol. Bring to a simmer and reduce until the liquid absorbs into the mushrooms. Season to taste with salt and pepper.

LOBSTER AND WILD MUSHROOM RISOTTO

1 pound Arborio rice (Italian short grain)
½ cup Maui onions, diced
¼ cup fennel, diced
¼ pound butter
1 cup shiitake mushrooms, sliced
2 quarts lobster or fish stock

½ cup oyster mushrooms, sliced
2 oz. parmesan cheese, grated
½ cup heavy cream
½ cup herbs, chopped (thyme, basil,
  rosemary, chives, parsley)

In a thick bottom sauce pot, sauté the onions and fennel in half the butter until they are golden brown. Add the rice and mushrooms; sauté for 3 to 5 minutes. Add 2 cups of stock at a time and bring to a simmer. When stock is absorbed by the rice, add another 2 cups of stock at a time until the stock is gone. Stir frequently while cooking the rice, which helps the risotto to become creamy. When the rice is tender, finish with the cheese, butter and cream. Season to taste with salt and pepper. Garnish the top of the risotto with the herbs and more cheese. To make into an entrée, add a grilled lobster tail with this dish.

Serves 5–8.

*T*ucked away in the quaint town of Makawao, you'll find the charming Courtyard Café. Near art galleries and a glass-blowing studio, the courtyard setting is lovely, breezy and centered around a magnificent Coral tree that offers a pleasing pattern of sunshine and shade. Inside the café, it is intimate and cozy with high ceilings and wooden furniture. This is where you place your order before you settle in.

Judith Hall, who has lived on Maui for 20 years, opened the Courtyard Café in 1997. Judith says, "I like to offer fresh, high quality food using the best ingredients." She also explained that it's important to have a staff that is happy, open and enjoys what they do, and it shows in the food.

Homebaked nine-grain bread, Heavenly Devil cookies and Blueberry–Mango or Strawberry–Peach Scones give an idea of what kind of yummy goodies can be found at the Courtyard Café. They make their own soups: Manhattan Chowder, Veggie Minestrone, Black Bean Chili. Popular fresh salads are: Ginger Sesame Tofu, Chicken Curry, and Fresh Green Bean Feta Sundried Tomato. Or, try a delicious Ono Sandwich. Breakfast items include Smoked Salmon Scramble; Belgian Waffle with fresh tropical fruit; and Spinach-Feta Omelet. On Sunday mornings, this is one of my favorite places to go for Ono Eggs Benedict (only available on Sunday).

Enjoy a latte, mocha or other coffee drink, a selection of fine teas and even fountain treats like an old fashioned root beer float.

Open daily. Breakfast and lunch under $10.00. Located at the Courtyard behind the Makawao Steak House.

HEAVENLY DEVIL COOKIES

4 eggs

1½ cups sugar

1 Tbsp. instant coffee

1 Tbsp. vanilla

6 oz. butter (1½ sticks)

4 oz. unsweetened chocolate

2 cups chocolate chips (to melt)

2 cups chocolate chips (leave unmelted)

2 cups flour

¼ tsp. salt

1 tsp. baking soda

3 cups chopped walnuts

Preheat oven to 325 degrees. Grease 2 cookie sheets and lightly flour. Mix eggs, sugar, coffee, and vanilla with a whisk. Melt butter and unsweetened chocolate over heat, stirring often, or microwave at 60% power. When the chocolate and butter are melted, add 2 cups of chocolate chips and continue until melted. Add melted chocolate to egg mix while whisking. Add flour, salt, and baking soda to the egg-chocolate mix and stir. Add 2 cups of unmelted chocolate chips and chopped walnuts. Stir with a spoon until mixed. Using an ice cream scoop, scoop onto a cookie sheet. Bake for approximately 18 minutes. Cookies will still be slightly soft. Do not over-bake.

Yields 18 cookies.

GINGER SESAME TOFU SALAD

1 block hard tofu, cut into chunks

2 cups shredded carrots

2 cups won bok (Chinese cabbage), chopped

1 red bell pepper, diced

8 oz. bean sprouts

½ cup green onion, chopped

½ cup toasted sesame seeds

DRESSING

⅛ cup sesame oil

⅛ cup salad oil

½ cup brown sugar

juice of one lime

1 cup soy sauce

1 cup orange juice

2 Tbsp. fresh ginger, chopped

Mix salad; pour the dressing over it and gently toss.

The owners and creative forces of Pacific'O, I'o and the Old Lahaina Luau have combined talents to create **The Feast at Lele**, an innovative venue that blends dynamic Luau performances with gourmet fine dining. Sitting outside by the beach at your own reserved table complete with white linens, you can experience the cultures and cuisines of Hawai`i, Tonga, Tahiti and Samoa. Each act is accompanied by a sampling of dishes representing the culture, which have been researched and created by Executive Chef James McDonald. *Travel & Leisure* says, "This is the most fabulous cooking on Maui, which is saying a lot."

Chef McDonald explains that as the sun is setting, a canoe brings performers in and a young native man carries a beautiful princess to the grass stage where she performs her hypnotic, erotic dance that mesmerizes and captures everyone's imagination. As you become entranced by the powerful music, chants and dance, you can enjoy fine wines, tropical drinks and outstanding dishes such as: Steamed Moi—fresh individual fish (this used to be served only to the Ali`i–Hawaiian royalty) garnished with crispy ono seaweed and tobiko caviar. From Tahiti: Fafa—chicken wrapped in taro leaf baked in coconut milk, chicken stock, ginger and lemongrass; and E`iaota-poisson cru. From Samoa: Shrimp and Avocado with lilikoi dressing, and more. Banana Coconut Haupia, Hawaiian Chocolate Truffles and tropical fruits are the finishing touches. Call for performance nights, prices and reservations.

E`IAOTA — POISSON CRU

1 ¼ pound white flesh fish file, diced (ono, mahimahi, hebi, monchong, etc.)

¼ cup English cucumber, peeled, seeded and medium dice

¼ cup tomato, medium dice

¼ cup carrot, julienne

¼ cup Maui onion, julienne

2 Tbsp. hot pepper, finely chopped

2 Tbsp. cilantro, chopped

1 cup lime juice

10 oz. coconut milk

salt and pepper

fresh lime, cut in wedges

Dice fish file into ½" cubes. Marinate for at least 3 to 4 hours in all of the lime juice in a steel container. (Fish should be covered with lime juice.) In a mixing bowl, add all remaining ingredients 20 to 30 minutes before fish is ready and toss together. Drain fish from marinade. Then add fish to salad, mix well; adjust seasoning, chill and serve. Garnish with lime wedge.

Serves 6.

PALUSAMI

5 cups breadfruit

1 cup onion, diced

2 Tbsp. butter

3 cups coconut milk

1 cup whole milk

2 cups taro leaf, chopped

salt and pepper

Roast breadfruit at 400 degrees for 45 minutes. Remove from oven and let cool. Peel skin, remove core and dice meat into 1" cubes. In 2 quart pot, sauté onions in butter on medium-high for 5 minutes. Add coconut milk, whole milk and one cup of taro leaf. Simmer on low for 20 minutes. Remove from heat and let cool. When cool, pour sauce into a blender; blend on high for 30 seconds. In a baking pan, arrange breadfruit, season with salt and pepper, and pour half of the sauce over breadfruit. Arrange remaining taro over breadfruit; then top with remaining sauce. Cover with aluminum foil and bake at 350 degrees for 1 hour. Remove from oven, serve hot.

Serves 6.

Chef's note: If taro leaf is not available, substitute spinach or other green leaf vegetable.

*A*s you approach Ferraro's at Seaside, live Italian music lures you into the romantic setting where you can relax with the soft lull of ocean waves and a sensuous breeze while the rich hues of the sunset spread out along the horizon. White linens, candle light and flaming tiki torches light up the night as stars emerge in the darkening sky.

In this enchanting environment, authentic Italian cuisine, fused with a contemporary flair, is the specialty show- casing items such as: Ravioli d'Anitra all'Essenza di Tartufo e Asparagi (duck ravioli, green asparagus with white truffle essence) and Tonno ai Sapori del Mediterraneo (pepper crusted 'ahi, tomato and kalamata olive ragout, orzo pasta). If you like dynam- ic flavor combi-

nations, try the antipasti Pomodori con Crostone (oven dried toma- toes, pesto sauce and goat cheese on country bread).

The wine list is superb and the attentive servers can suggest the right wine to enhance each course coordinating with Italy's geographic regions. Complete your experience with Semifreddo al Gianduja e Moscato, Salsa al Pistachio (moscato scented chocolate–hazelnut mousse with pistachio sauce) or one of the other fine dessert choices and a coffee drink or Italian after dinner drink.

Lunch serves casual fare for $8.50–17.00. Dinner appetizers: $9.00–14.50, entrées: $21.50–32.00. A special chef's menu is also offered. Open daily. Live instrumental duo nightly. Call for reservations.

IL CARPACCIO DI MANZO CON CARCIOFINI MARINATI, SALSA VERDE
BEEF CARPACCIO WITH ARTICHOKE, GREEN SAUCE IN A BED OF BABY MIXED GREENS

2 oz. thinly sliced beef tenderloin

2 oz. parsley

½ oz. corn scions

1 Tbsp. vinegar

1 slice white bread

1 hard-boiled egg yolk

½ oz. capers

½ oz. onion

2 oz. olive oil

1 oz. marinated artichoke

1 oz. baby mixed greens

1 oz. shaved parmesan cheese

salt and pepper to taste

For dressing: mix ingredients listed from parsley through olive oil; add salt and pepper. Combine the mixed greens with the dressing. Top with beef; spread with more dressing, add artichokes, and finish with parmesan cheese.

TONNO AI SAPORI DEL MEDITERRANEO
PEPPERED `AHI TUNA, TOMATO AND OLIVES, ORZO PASTA

5 oz. tuna "`ahi" steak

1 Tbsp. Dijon mustard

1 oz. crushed black peppercorn

1½ oz. spinach

1½ oz. oven dried tomatoes

½ oz. kalamata olives

2 oz. orzo pasta

1 tsp. chopped parsley

1 oz. olive oil

salt and pepper to taste

Coat the `ahi with Dijon mustard, then the black pepper, then sear and finish on the grill until medium rare. Sauté the spinach with olive oil. Add salt and pepper. Cut the tomato in cubes and sauté with olive oil and kalamata olives. Cook the orzo in boiling water for 10 minutes. Sauté with olive oil, parsley, salt and pepper. Make a crow on the plate alternating spinach and tomato. Place the orzo in the middle of the plate, topped with the `ahi.

As a true artist who uses food as his medium, Gerard Reversade has been recognized for over 15 years as one of the leading chefs in the state of Hawai`i. He has received numerous awards and was recently featured on two major television shows: "Country Cooking" on P.B.S. and "Great Chefs of America" on the Discovery Channel.

Born in the Gascony region of France, Chef Gerard began gardening, cooking and baking as a young boy. When he was 14, he started an apprenticeship with 4 master chefs of France.

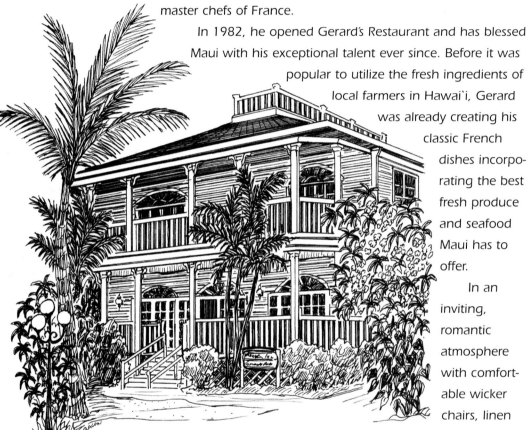

In 1982, he opened Gerard's Restaurant and has blessed Maui with his exceptional talent ever since. Before it was popular to utilize the fresh ingredients of local farmers in Hawai`i, Gerard was already creating his classic French dishes incorporating the best fresh produce and seafood Maui has to offer.

In an inviting, romantic atmosphere with comfortable wicker chairs, linen tablecloths and stained glass windows, you can choose to dine on the porch or inside where you will be surrounded with French country Victorian charm. The service is outstanding, as is the artfully presented food and exceptional wine list.

Favorites include the Grilled Rack of Lamb in mint crust—roasted garlic, eggplant charlotte and potato au gratin and the Roasted Hawaiian Snapper with star anise, fennel fondue, and emulsion of orange and ginger. Gerard offers a seductive dessert menu with Pineapple or Mango Tarte Tatin—fruit of the season baked in a flaky pastry tart served warm with ice cream, and Macadamia Nut Chocolate Cake with chestnut chantilly cream and cappuccino sauce, and there's much more to allure you.

Dinner nightly. Entrées from $26.50. Reservations recommended.

CHICKEN WITH GARLIC, MAUI ONIONS, TOMATO AND BELL PEPPER, BASQUAISE STYLE

1 chicken cut into 8 pieces

4 large green, red and yellow bell peppers

¼ cup olive oil

2 garlic cloves, peeled and sliced

1 large Maui onion, sliced

4 large tomatoes, peeled, seeded and coarsely cut into chunks

½ Hawaiian hot pepper, seeded and finely chopped

1 bouquet garni—tie together:

2 sprigs fresh thyme

2 sprigs basil leaves

1 bay leaf

Put the bell peppers over a flame until the skin puffs up. Place them into a paper bag and let them steam for a few minutes. Peel and core the bell peppers and cut them into large strips. In a heavy large pan, heat the oil, add the garlic and sauté for a few seconds, then add the onions, peppers, tomatoes, Hawaiian pepper and bouquet garni. Cover and simmer for 30 minutes.

In a separate sauté pan, cook the chicken in olive oil, season with salt and pepper. Cook for about 30 minutes. When done transfer onto a platter and cover with the above sauce. Serve with rice or french fries.

MANGO JAM

2 pounds mangoes

1½ pounds sugar, preferably sugar cubes

1 vanilla bean

1 star anise

lemon zest

Cut the mangoes in even pieces, macerate overnight with sugar, spices and lemon zest. The next day, cook, stirring often, until jelly stage. (220F.)

*A*s you drive through the beautiful pastureland of Upcountry Maui through Kula on your way to Ulapalakua, you will pass through the quaint, charming town of Keokea. White churches, a park, a couple of neighborhood stores, a gallery and Grandma's Coffee House complete the town.

Inspired by his grandmother and the many generations in his family who have grown and processed coffee, Alfred Franco opened Grandma's Coffee House in 1988. His grandmother, who is now in her nineties, taught Al about growing, harvesting, processing and even drinking coffee, and she gave him her blessing to continue with the family tradition.

The coffee beans used to make Grandma's Coffee are organically grown in Upcountry Maui on several small farms

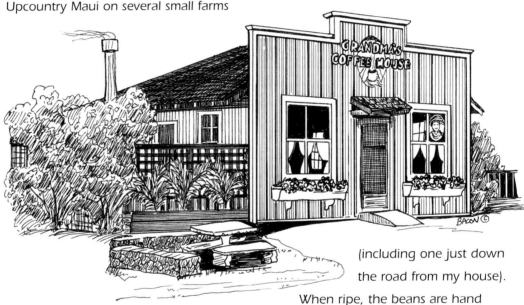

(including one just down the road from my house).

When ripe, the beans are hand picked, and Al roasts them using an 1885 roasting machine that has been in his family for many years. You can purchase the coffee by the pound at Grandma's or on the internet at grandmascoffee.com, or call 1-800-375-7853.

Grandma's Coffee House is small and friendly, with wooden floors and a new deck area that takes advantage of the expansive Upcountry view looking out over Maui and the endless ocean. It's a great place to enjoy a Belgium Waffle with tropical fruit in season, or for lunch try a Taro Burger, BLT sandwich, Lasagna, Pasta or Potato salad. A changing selection of goodies include: Carrot Cake, Banana Mango Bread, Cherry, Peach or Apple Cobbler, and a Pineapple Banana Mac Nut Cake that is incredible. Or with a smoothie, cappuccino or mocha, try a cheesecake or Tiramisu.

Under $10.00. Open daily 7 a.m. to 5 p.m.

AL'S ORIENTAL BBQ CHICKEN

5 pounds chicken thighs

1½ cups your favorite BBQ sauce

1¼ cups brown sugar

3 Tbsp. sesame oil

4 oz. fresh Hawaiian ginger, chopped

3 tsp. black pepper

4 cloves garlic, chopped

¼ cup green onions, chopped

½ cup oyster sauce

toasted sesame seeds

Mix all ingredients (except chicken) together. Marinate chicken for 1 hour in the BBQ mixture. Pour all into a baking dish. Bake at 350 degrees for approximately 45 minutes to 1 hour until done. Sprinkle with toasted sesame seeds and garnish with green onions.

MAUI PINEAPPLE COCONUT SQUARES

Crust:

½ cup butter, melted

½ cup sugar

2 cups flour

1 tsp. baking powder

2 egg yolks

Middle layer:

1 – 16 oz. can crushed pineapple, drained

Topping:

1½ cups packed, flaked coconut

1 cup sugar

½ cup pineapple juice

1 tsp. butter

1 tsp. vanilla

3 egg whites

Mix crust ingredients with mixer for 2 minutes. Spread in a greased 9x13" pan. Bake at 325 degrees for 10 to 15 minutes, until golden brown.

Spread crushed pineapple on cooked crust. Mix topping ingredients in bowl. When well mixed, add whipped egg whites. Mix well. Spread evenly over pineapple. Bake at 350 degrees for 30 to 35 minutes.

*I*n an atmosphere that is tropical and hip and just steps from the beach, guests of **Hula Grill** can experience the exceptional talent of Chef Peter Merriman (see page 180). One of the founders of Hawai'i Regional Cuisine—a group of chefs dedicated to working with farmers and utilizing fresh local ingredients—Merriman combined talents with TS Restaurants to open Hula Grill in 1994. A favorite on Maui, Hula Grill is a Hale 'Aina award-winner for 1999 and 2000.

The building that houses Hula Grill was designed to be like an old Kama'aina beach house and displays many architectural elements from times past. With white columns and an open beam ceiling supporting 2 solid koa canoes overhead, the restaurant offers open-air seating, a view of the glistening ocean, passing boats and parasailors backed by Lana'i and Molokai'i.

Popular menu items include: Wok Charred 'Ahi; Fire Cracker Mahimahi served with black bean, Maui onion and avocado relish; Puna Goat Cheese, Macadamia Nut and Shrimp Quesadilla; and BBQ Pork Spare Ribs. The favorite dessert is the Homemade Ice Cream Sandwich: vanilla ice cream, macadamia nut brownies, raspberry sauce and whipped cream. So good!

Open daily. Lunch: $7.95–12.95. Dinner entrées: $14.95–24.95. Live contemporary music and hula dancers in the evening.

The Barefoot Bar, complete with sand floor, grass thatched umbrellas and patrons who may be bikini clad and dripping from a dip in the ocean (the slogan is: no shoes, no shirt, no problem,) serves drinks and pupus from 11 a.m. to 11 p.m. daily.

PINEAPPLE SALSA

1 cup vine ripened tomatoes

½ cup Maui onions

2 fresh jalepeño peppers

½ Tbsp. chopped garlic

1 Tbsp. coriander seed, crushed

1 Tbsp. cumin, crushed

1 Tbsp. kosher salt

2 cups vine ripened tomatoes, diced

½ cup Maui onions, diced

¼ cup cilantro, diced

2 cups fresh pineapple, diced

Purée first 7 ingredients; then add diced ingredients and mix well.

PINEAPPLE COLESLAW

2 pounds green cabbage, shredded

¼ pound red cabbage, shredded

6 Tbsp. carrots, shredded

3 Tbsp. cilantro, chopped

½ cup red onion, sliced

½ fresh pineapple, diced

3 Tbsp. rice wine vinegar

3 Tbsp. sugar

1 Tbsp. black sesame seeds

3 Tbsp. soy sauce

3 Tbsp. fresh ginger, peeled and chopped

3 Tbsp. sesame seed oil

3 Tbsp. champagne vinegar

Combine the first 6 ingredients and reserve. Combine the remaining ingredients and mix well. Mix the two together thoroughly.

HUMUHUMUNUKUNUKUAPUA`A

Unique and exceptional, **Humuhumunukunukuapua`a** is extremely high on the list of best places to enjoy a romantic sunset dinner. The setting is spectacular with the sunset reflecting on the shimmering lagoon and ocean, accented by silhouetted palm trees and glowing tiki torches. This restaurant with the intimidating name (it's actually simple once you get the rhythm of it) is named after the Hawai`i state fish and can be referred to as "Humuhumu." When entering Humuhumu, you cross over a wooden bridge by a lit waterfall and are led to see its namesake in an aquarium filled with tropical fish.

The open-air thatched roof wooden structure floats on a saltwater lagoon filled with tropical fish and Hawaiian lobster, which could end up on your dinner plate. You can participate in choosing and hoisting up your lobster in a cage with a rope and pulley assisted by the friendly waitstaff who offer their aloha.

The Crispy Lobster-Shrimp Cake with Waterchestnuts and Shiitake Mushrooms is outstanding! My companion and I followed that with the delicious Lemongrass and Lobster Veloute with Rock Shrimp and Coconut Milk, which was a tremendous lead-up to the incredible fresh Hawaiian Spiny Lobster. (So much lobster! So decadent and so good.) Three preparations are offered; we chose to have it grilled with Hawaiian salt, garlic and a lime chili butter served with chili pepper and shoyu. It was ambrosial—fit for the gods—the presentation, the flavors, the setting, and enhanced by a great bottle of wine. And, as if that is not enough, I'd recommend the Hawaiian Vintage Chocolate Tart with a lilikoi sorbet, raspberry coulis and a light caramel sauce.

Dinner nightly. Entrées start at $26.00. Reservations recommended.

LOBSTER WATERCHESTNUT CAKE

6 oz. Maine lobster, cooked
6 oz. rock shrimp, chopped
6 oz. fresh waterchestnuts
2 eggs
4 oz. mayonnaise
juice from one lemon
Worcestershire sauce to taste
Tabasco to taste

salt to taste
1 Tbsp. Dijon mustard
1 Tbsp. chives, chopped
1 tsp. parsley, chopped
6 oz. white bread, cubed
Wailea spice blend to taste
panko (Japanese bread crumbs)

Chop shrimp finely. Roughly chop lobster. Mix all seafood together. In another bowl, mix mayonnaise with all ingredients except white bread and panko. Season to taste. Mix in seafood; then fold in cubed bread. Let mix set for 2 hours in refrigerator. Form in 2 to 3 ounce patties. Coat in panko. Heat olive oil in a Teflon pan and sauté until crispy. Garnish with pickled mango and calamansi lime.

Yields 12 lobster cakes.

HUMUHUMUNUKUNUKUAPUA`A'S HAWAIIAN `AHI TARTAR

12 oz. fresh Hawaiian `ahi, diced
3 oz. Maui onions, diced

4 oz. cucumbers, diced
1 oz. toasted sesame seeds

LIME SHOYU SAUCE

4 oz. Dijon mustard
½ oz. lime juice
1 oz. rice vinegar
1 oz. mushroom soy sauce

1 tsp. sugar
1 tsp. sesame oil
1 tsp. fresh ginger, chopped

Dice all vegetables and `ahi. Toss together. Mix all lime shoyu sauce ingredients together. Lightly toss `ahi with lime sauce. Serve instantly with cucumber namasu, pickled ginger and crisp wonton chips.

Touted as "The Current Star" of Maui restaurants in *Travel & Leisure* magazine (November 1999), **I'o**, created by Pacific'O (see page 128) partners Executive Chef James McDonald, Louis Coulombe and Stephan Bel-Robert, is hip and cutting edge, offering Chef James an outlet for his creative ingenuity to reach even greater heights. The futuristic, post-modern-funk look was specifically designed and hand-crafted and is combined with a chic sophisticated feeling that you'd be likely to find in New York or San Francisco. Yet here it is on Maui and, like Pacific'O right next door, it's just steps from the beach. Chef James describes I'o as "exciting, exotic and adventurous, yet maintaining a level of quality and class that any five star restaurant should offer, with a staff that is knowledgeable, not stuffy." He said it well—my experience matches his description.

The non-obtrusive exhibition kitchen is highlighted behind lit etched-glass panels and the curved custom "Martini" bar is an artistic showpiece—as is Chef McDonald's food. The Silken Purse wonton appetizer is smooth and flavorful. Another excellent choice is the I'o Crabcake with puna goat cheese and Maui onion miso dressing. "The Box" is fabulous with melt-in-your-mouth fish. Entrées to try include Crispy `Ahi in a nori and panko crust with green papaya salad; or Lemongrass Coconut Fish. The Chocolate Paté for dessert is rich and wonderful and is complemented with a passion fruit anglaise and fresh Kula strawberries.

Whether you choose to sit outside under the stars, with the tropical ocean breezes, or inside the innovative open-air restaurant, you are sure to have a memorable experience.

Dinner served nightly. Entrées: $18.00–57.00. Call for reservations. Find them on the web at www.iomaui.com.

I'O

(808) 661-8422 • 505 Front Street, Lahaina, Maui 96761

SEAFOOD COCKTAIL

2 oz. shrimp, chopped
2 oz. fish scrap, shaved thin slices
2 oz. scallops
¾ cup lime juice
½ cup pineapple, dice large
½ cup papaya, dice large
½ cup mango, dice large
¼ cup red bell pepper, julienne
¼ cup Maui onion, julienne

2 Tbsp. cilantro, chopped
2 Tbsp. green olives, sliced
2 Tbsp. black olives, sliced
1 Tbsp. capers
Chipotle Tomatillo Sauce (recipe follows)
Sweet Potato Chips
lime wedges for garnish
salt and pepper

Marinate seafoods in lime juice for at least 2 hours. Mix fruits and vegetables with seafood. Season, add cilantro. Place in big margarita glass with lime wedges and cilantro sprigs.

CHIPOTLE TOMATILLO SAUCE

2 chipotle
4 oz. tomatillos
1 oz. garlic cloves
3 oz. onion

2 cups water
salt
3 oz. tomato

Place all in pot and simmer. Purée in blender and chill.

CHOCOLATE PATE WITH PASSION FRUIT ANGLAISE AND FRESH STRAWBERRIES

6 oz. unsalted butter
3½ pounds dark chocolate
3¾ cups heavy cream

1 cup powdered sugar
15 egg yolks
5 oz. dark rum (optional)

To make paté, place butter, chocolate and heavy cream in a bowl set over boiling water and melt together. Turn off heat and incorporate the powdered sugar followed by the yolks and finally the rum. Strain through a chinois into a buttered terrine lined with parchment paper. Chill overnight.

PASSION FRUIT ANGLAISE

1 vanilla bean, split, seeded
1 qt. milk
1 cup passion fruit purée
6 oz. egg yolks
8 oz. sugar
1½ oz. cornstarch

For garnish:
1 pint strawberries, stemmed, quartered
½ cup macadamia nuts, chopped

Place vanilla, milk and passion fruit purée into a sauce pot and bring to a scalding temperature. Mix egg yolk with sugar and cornstarch. Ladel ½ of the scalded liquid into the egg mix to temper and pour back into pot. Cook over medium heat until thickened. Whisk continuously and do not over cook or sauce will curdle. Remove from heat, pour through chinois and chill overnight.

To plate: Remove paté from terrine by dipping into hot water to loosen paper. Slice with hot knife or fishing line. Spoon some Anglaise on plate. Place a slice of paté on top and a spoonfull of strawberries; then sprinkle with macadamia nuts.

Jacques Bistro is located on the wild North shore where rainbows are frequently seen, and the quaint historic plantation town of Pa`ia is bustling with local residents. Just two miles away, Ho`okipa Beach offers world-class windsurfing drawing an international crowd, many of whom you will find at Jacques after a day riding the waves.

As they say at Jacques, "You can find a Bistro in New York, Paris or London, but here it's a Bistro filled with island life. People come here to meet with friends or find new ones, share a meal and to be entertained. It's a place where you can come alone and you are not going to feel alone. The specialty of the Bistro is not only the food, it's the atmosphere of fun and light heartedness. Come join us for a wonderful taste of Maui." And many on Maui have—*The Maui News Dining Guide* voted Jacques Bistro "Best Value" in 1998 and 1999; and they were honored with a 1999 *Zagat Survey* award.

Born in the South of France, Chef Jacques Pauvert graduated from a top culinary school in France. Then he traveled, lived and cooked in many different places until settling down on Maui and opening Jacques Bistro in 1998 and sister restaurant, Jacques on the Beach in 1999.

Favorite dishes include: Fresh Grilled Fish prepared special each evening; Grilled Rack of Lamb with cranberry apricot glaze and roasted garlic; and Jacques Seafood Bowl—fresh fish and shell fish prepared bouillabaisse style with a Hawaiian French touch. Most dinners are served with potatoes, rice, fresh Kula vegetables and a basket of fresh baked bread.

Open nightly. Dinners: $9.95–23.95. Call for reservations.

JACQUES BISTRO

(808) 579-6255 • 89 Hana Highway, Pa`ia, Maui 96779

DUCK CONFIT

2 duck legs

1 bay leaf

whole peppercorns (to taste)

½ cup pineapple chunks

orange zest

Place 2 duck legs (per person, multiply ingredients per servings) in a roasting pan. Coat with duck fat drippings, lard or canola oil. Add bay leaves, whole peppercorns, pineapple chunks and orange zest. Cover with aluminum foil and bake at 300 degrees for 4 hours. Serve with sauce:

½ cup rice vinegar

pineapple chunks

½ cup white wine

1 tsp. orange zest

cornstarch

Mix all ingredients together and cook in a saucepan over a low flame. Add cornstarch mixed with water to thicken to desired consistency.

TRADITIONAL CREME BRULEE

1 quart heavy cream

5 whole Tahitian vanilla beans, split in half

10 egg yolks

1 cup sugar

Bring to boil the cream and vanilla beans in a medium saucepan. Remove from heat and let cool. In a separate bowl, whisk the egg yolks with sugar until thick. Stir in the heavy cream mixture. Ladle the mixture into ceramic dishes. Arrange the dishes in a bain–marie of cold water halfway up the sides of the dishes. Set the bain–marie in a 300 degree oven and bake for 1 hour or until set.

*J*acques on the Beach in Kihei offers many of the same delightful Bistro qualities that are enjoyed at Jacques Bistro in Pa`ia with the added romance of spectacular views of Lana`i, Kahoolawe and the West Maui Mountains. In an open-air setting you will be seduced by romantic sunsets, whales (in season) and the charm of being served near the water.

Following the success of sister restaurant Jacques Bistro (see previous page), Jacques on the Beach was voted Best Value 1999 and Best New Restaurant 1999, honorable mention; and Best Overall 1999, honorable mention by *The Maui News Dining Guide.*

You can relax with a glass of wine and enjoy the ocean view and experience the same great value and tastefully prepared fresh food as you'll find at Jacques in Pa`ia. A sample of menu items includes tasty appetizers and salads: Tomato Mozzarella Salad—slices of fresh mozzarella imported from Italy, layered with sliced tomatoes, a balsamic dressing with chopped fresh basil, ground pepper and Kula greens; and Island Sashimi—fresh raw fish served on a bed of shredded cabbage with one-scoop rice, Kula greens and wasabi mustard and shoyu. Dinners feature fresh seafood, steak, chicken, ribs and more. Seafood Linguini is served with fresh island fish, prawns, mussels and calamari in Jacques's ciopinno style sauce of tomatoes, garlic, wine and fresh herbs. Most dinners are served with potatoes, rice, fresh Kula vegetables and a basket of fresh baked bread.

Open nightly. Dinners: $9.95–23.95. Call for reservations.

HANA ROAD SALAD

8 cups organic Kula mixed greens
  (or comparable)

½ pound smoked salmon, diced

2 apples, diced

½ pound havarti cheese, diced

croutons

Mix together and toss with Raspberry Vinaigrette and croutons.
Serves 6.

RASPBERRY VINAIGRETTE

¼ cup fresh or frozen raspberries

½ cup raspberry vinegar

½ cup olive oil

½ cup canola oil

1 Tbsp. water

fresh tarragon, salt and pepper to taste

Purée raspberries in a blender and mix with other ingredients.

PAN FRIED MAHIMAHI

4 mahimahi fillets

4 pieces day-old bread

1 Tbsp. coarse ground garlic

fresh parsley

Grill bread in oven; then grind in blender with parsley and garlic. Coat both sides of
mahimahi with breadcrumb mixture. Place in a very hot sauté pan and sauté each side of
fish for less than 1 minute. Finish baking the mahimahi in a 350 degree oven for approximately 6 minutes. Serve with vinaigrette sauce:

¼ cup sundried tomatoes

½ cup balsamic vinegar

8 leaves fresh basil

½ cup extra virgin olive oil

ground pepper to taste

Mix all ingredients together and add a splash of water.
Makes 4 servings.

*C*ondé Nast Traveler calls Lahaina Coolers the "Cheers" of the Pacific (where everybody knows your name . . .) It's a friendly place for the community where people know each other; visitors enjoy the spot also and often will return on their next trip.

Owners Steve Whiston and Dan Dull did a beautiful job remodeling the restaurant with hardwood floors, teak chairs, flowered tablecloths, and local artists' work featured on the walls. Seating is available indoors where surf and dive videos play silently for visual entertainment while accompanied by music; outside you can stay cool from the heat of Lahaina with misters softly spraying cool droplets of water.

Steve explains that they like to offer "wonderful Hawai`i regional flavors at an affordable price." Many daily specials are featured including a homemade ravioli dish, a fresh pasta selection, and a wine. The fresh catch on the specials page tells the name of the captain, boat and how many pounds the fish weighed in at. An example of a preparation: Fresh Opakapaka with soy-lime-ginger buerre blanc. Hand-tossed pizza, their signature, Evil Jungle Pasta, and Hawaiian Style Pork Ribs are also popular choices. There's even a daily dessert, which may be something like White Chocolate Raspberry Cheesecake.

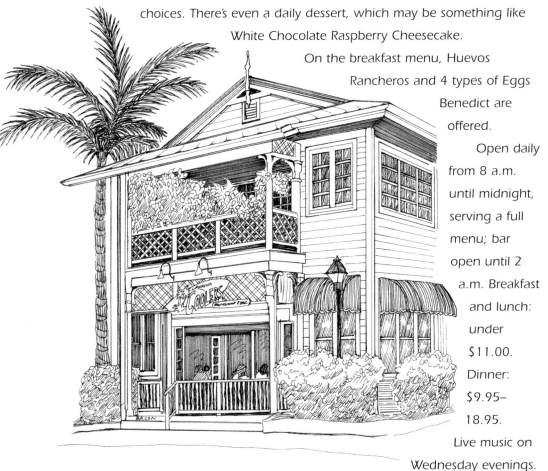

On the breakfast menu, Huevos Rancheros and 4 types of Eggs Benedict are offered.

Open daily from 8 a.m. until midnight, serving a full menu; bar open until 2 a.m. Breakfast and lunch: under $11.00. Dinner: $9.95–18.95.

Live music on Wednesday evenings.

SPICY AZTECA

3 oz. chicken breast

1 oz. bacon, cooked

2 oz. tomato, diced

1 tsp. garlic, chopped

3 oz. white wine

1 Tbsp. whole butter

1 tsp. chipotle
   pepper, minced

1 oz. cilantro, chopped

7 oz. linguine

parmesan cheese and cilantro for garnish

Cook pasta in boiling water. In a heated sauté pan, cook chicken, tomato, and garlic until chicken is done. Deglaze with white wine. Add butter, peppers and cilantro. Reduce by half. Toss with drained pasta and serve in pasta bowl. Garnish with fresh cilantro and parmesan cheese.

SIZZLING GARLIC SHRIMP

15 shrimp, peeled and deveined

¼ cup garlic, sliced

2 Tbsp. olive oil

1 dash chili paste

1 pinch kosher salt

parsley, chopped

fresh lemon wedges

Mix salt and prawns in a bowl. Mix olive oil, chili paste and garlic. Place garlic–oil mixture in a pre-heated iron skillet. Cook garlic on high heat until edges of garlic are brown in color. Place shrimp evenly on iron skillet and cover. Cook on high heat until shrimp are pink on the outside and opaque in the center. Garnish with chopped parsley and fresh lemon wedges.

*L*ocated at the beautiful Kea Lani Hotel, Nick's Fishmarket Maui has been recognized with accolades both nationwide and locally, and they were honored with the 2000 Hale `Aina award. Blending Maui's natural beauty with the romance of a Mediterranean villa, Nick's features an open-air setting where you may dine inside in a booth just for two, or be romanced under stars and vine-covered trellises. Or, for a more casual moment to enjoy an appetizer and drink, try the curving granite bar.

A spectacular 800-gallon aquarium is one of the unique features of the restaurant, along with a glass-enclosed 2,000 bottle wine display with fine vintages from Italy, France, Germany and California. In 1999, Nick's Fishmarket Maui was honored with an Ilima Award for Dining Excellence as the "Best New Restaurant in Hawai`i." It is the third successful restaurant in Hawai`i for restaurateur, Aaron Placourakis and Tri–Star Restaurant Group.

Innovative, classic cuisine with fresh seafood is the primary focus of Nick's menu, featuring items such as: Live Maine and Hawaiian Lobster, Fresh Opakapaka, `Ahi, California Abalone and Prime Steaks. Preparations include Fresh Opah seasoned with

basil and a citrus aioli and baked in phyllo, and a Blackened Mahimahi—cajun crusted, seared and finished with a cayenne lobster sauce. Dinner served nightly. Entrées from $24.95. Call for reservations. Valet parking.

Sister restaurants are Aaron's Atop the Ala Moana, page 58, and Sarento's Top of the "I" page 90.

GREEK MAUI WOWIE SALAD

1 avocado, diced medium

2 vine ripened tomatoes, diced medium

1 cup Maui onion, peeled and diced small

2 cups rock shrimp, poached in lobster stock and cooled

2 oz. feta cheese, grated fine

4 cups romaine lettuce, sliced

4 peperconi (Greek peppers)

8 kalamata olives, pitted

8 oz. Nick's Dressing (see below)

8 oz. Greek Dressing (see below)

Place 2 ounces of Greek Dressing on each plate in the center of the plate. In mixing bowl, put avocado, tomato, onion, shrimp, ½ the feta cheese, romaine and all of Nick's Dressing. Toss lightly, then place on top of the Greek Dressing. Garnish with remaining feta cheese and 2 kalamata and 1 peperconi pepper each.

Serves 4. (Other options include adding cooked lobster meat and cucumbers.)

GREEK DRESSING

½ cup mayonnaise

1 tsp. fresh mint, chopped

1 tsp. Greek oregano

¼ tsp. garlic, chopped

1 tsp. Worcestershire sauce

1 tsp. E.V.O. olive oil

1 Tbsp. red wine vinegar

Mix all together in a bowl with a whisk.

NICK'S DRESSING

¼ cup roasted red peppers, peeled, seeded, and diced small

2 Tbsp. capers

1 tsp. hard boiled egg white, grated

1 tsp. Italian parsley, chopped

1 pinch black pepper and salt

1 Tbsp. red wine vinegar

1 Tbsp. canola oil

2 Tbsp. olive oil

1 tsp. Dijon mustard

1 dash tabasco

Mix all together in a bowl with a whisk.

*I*n a beautifully comfortable environment surrounded by orchids, plumeria and palm trees, you can drink in the splendor of the magnificent grounds of Four Seasons Resort. With ocean and West Maui mountain views, intriguing pool-side cabanas, a warm atmosphere and a friendly staff, a wonderful, refined and tropical ambiance is created at Pacific Grill. You may choose to dine outside or in the open-air dining room.

Bountiful breakfast buffets include tropical fruits, omelettes made to order, pastries and much more; breakfast menu items are also served. For dinner, I found the Crisped Shutome with sweet miso ginger sauce had incredible flavor! You can also choose Stir Fry Beef or Mango-Lime Huli Huli Chicken. Enjoy a great selection of wines to complement your meal and save room for dessert—the Caramelized Banana Cream (flourless chocolate cake and coconut milk) is outrageous, unique and delicious. A Hawaiian duet adds to the ambiance on select evenings.

Breakfast served daily: $9.25–24.50, buffet: $18.25–22.50. Dinner served nightly. Appetizers: $8.00–10.50; entrées: $18.50–29.50. Call for reservations.

SLIPPER LOBSTER SPRING ROLLS, JAPANESE PICKLES, SWEET CHILI SAUCE

SPRING ROLLS

3 oz. slipper lobster meat, diced

1 oz. each garlic shallot and ginger, minced

1 oz. shiitake mushrooms, julienne

1 oz. glass noodles, cooked, cooled

1 oz. carrots, julienne

1 oz. Chinese cabbage, julienne

1 oz. green onion, chopped

1 oz. cilantro, chopped

1 oz. cornstarch

1 pkg. lumpia wrappers

egg wash

assorted Japanese pickled vegetables

Sauté lobster meat with garlic, shallots, and ginger over medium heat. Dust with cornstarch. Chill. Mix all ingredients. Wrap in lumpia wrapper and seal with egg wash. Arrange 3 rolls with sauce on a rectangular ceramic. Tie rolls with ti leaf. Garnish with Japanese pickled vegetables.

SWEET CHILI SAUCE

1 Tbsp. sweet Thai garlic

1 Tbsp. rice wine vinegar

1 tsp. Thai chili garlic

Mix all ingredients together.

BARBEQUE CHINESE STYLE RIBS, PINEAPPLE COLE SLAW

RIBS

1 case pork ribs, peeled

2 lbs. mire poix

Simmer ribs with sachet and mire poix with enough water to cover. Skim and simmer for 3 hours, until tender.

SACHET

½ cup star anise

10 each lemongrass

2 oz. pepper flakes

1 cup ginger, peeled

4 oz. Thai chili garlic

2 oz. garlic

4 each bay leaf

Tie all ingredients in a cheese cloth.

BARBEQUE SAUCE

2 cups Hoisin

6 oz. red pepper purée

4 oz. shoyu marinade

2 Tbsp. chili garlic

1 Tbsp. crystallized ginger, minced

1 Tbsp. ginger, minced

Mix all ingredients together.

PINEAPPLE COLE SLAW

1 head white cabbage, julienne

2 carrots, julienne

1 pineapple, diced

2 oz. cilantro

2 oz. red wine vinegar

4 oz. mayonnaise

Mix all ingredients together and serve with ribs.

*I*nnovative, chic and cutting edge are words that describe both Chef James McDonald and his food. Along with the award-winning Pacific'O, this talented executive chef and his partners Louis Coulombe and Stephan Bel-Robert have two more venues that are receiving rave reviews: I'o (see page 116) and Feast at Lele (see page 104).

Pacific'O has been recognized with many awards including: *Wine Spectator's* "Award of Excellence and " A Taste of Lahaina "Best Seafood." Chef McDonald was honored with *The Maui News* "Best Maui Chef" award. He is the "poster child" for Maui Community College's food service program; he has traveled as a culinary representative for the Hawai`i Visitor's Bureau, has received international recognition and brought a taste of Hawai`i to Japan, London and to passengers on board a luxury cruise ship.

Chef James says he likes to keep his food "light and fresh with the emphasis on fresh fish and blending the different cultures of the islands." Inspired by local products, he does a lot of research and continually looks for new ways to utilize fresh ingredients. Everything is made from scratch, including delicious breads that are baked daily.

At Pacific'O, you can sit just steps from the waves rolling along the golden sand as the sun sets over Lana`i and be treated to spectacular and flavorful dishes such as: Fresh `Ahi and Ono Tempura with white miso dressing and lime basil sauce; Coconut Macadamia Nut Crusted Catch of the day with Thai peanut coconut sauce, sweet and sour glaze and tropical fruit salsa. The award-winning Prawn and Basil Won Ton appetizer, and Roasted Maui Onion and Big Island Puna Goat Cheese Salad are a tasty way to begin. Try the incredible Banana Pineapple Lumpia for dessert.

Open daily for lunch and dinner. Dinner entrées: $19.00–28.00. Reservations recommended. Visit them on the web at www.pacificomaui.com.

PACIFIC'O (808) 667-4341 • 505 Front Street, Lahaina, Maui 96761

SEARED FRESH FISH WITH MACADAMIA COCONUT CRUST, THAI PEANUT SAUCE & SWEET N' SOUR GLAZE

4 fresh fish fillets, 8 oz. each

8 oz. macadamia nuts, whole or chopped

2 oz. coconut, unsweetened, untoasted, long thread preferred

salt and pepper to taste

1 egg, lightly whipped (for dipping)

½ cup flour (for dusting)

2 oz. peanut/sesame oil, mix

steamed rice

For salsa garnish, chop and mix:

mangoes

pineapple

papaya

fresh cilantro

Maui Onions

Place macadamia nuts in a food processor and grind until coarse. (You may need to add some coconut to assist the grinding.) Remove to a pan or plate and mix with coconut. Season fish fillets; dip one side in flour, then in eggs, then in the nut mix. Heat a sauté pan with the oil to medium high and place fish into pan, nut side down. Be careful not to blacken the nuts. Turn the fish and continue cooking until fish is desired temperature. (If using 'ahi, it is at its best when rare to medium rare.) Remove from pan and place on a bed of steamed rice. Ladel Peanut Sauce around the fish and Sweet n' Sour Glaze over the fish. Top with garnish.

SWEET N' SOUR GLAZE

1 cup sugar

1 cup red wine vinegar

1 oz. soy sauce

1 tsp. crushed chili flakes

1 Tbsp. ground cinnamon

Place all ingredients in a sauce pot; bring to a boil. Reduce heat; simmer for 20 minutes. Sauce should be served hot over fish and may be reserved in the refrigerator indefinitely.

THAI PEANUT SAUCE

8 oz. coconut milk

8 oz. chicken broth

½ cup creamy peanut butter

1 stalk lemongrass, smashed and chopped (may substitute lemon zest)

1 oz. bulb fresh ginger, smashed

4 cloves garlic, smashed

1 tsp. Chinese chili paste

½ tsp. cornstarch combined with:

juice of 1 lime and salt to taste

Heat a sauce pot with lemongrass, garlic and ginger, stirring continuously for approximately one minute to release oils. Next add chicken broth, coconut milk and peanut butter. Boil for 20 minutes; add chili paste, salt and cornstarch/lime juice mix. Remove from heat and strain.

From it's unique majestic vantage point in the hills of Kapalua, **The Plantation House** creates a relaxing plantation-style environment to take in fine food, wine and a spectacular sunset over the Kapalua coast and Moloka`i. Situated on the

Plantation Course at Kapalua, the restaurant is surrounded by soft emerald hills that glow in the late afternoon sun, and on chilly winter nights, the cozy fireplace in the dining room creates a soft romantic glow inside.

Executive Chef Alex Stanislaw was voted Best Chef 1999 by the readers of *The Maui News*. "There's a lot of passion and emotion involved with food," he says and explains that he likes to create real, homey comfort food (much needed in our busy lives) using fresh local ingredients and bold intense flavors. Fresh fish preparations include: "A Taste of the Mediterranean," Maui onion mustard crusted fish on oven roasted Maui onions with fried caper sauce; and "The Asian Pacific" sesame-crusted fish on a soba noodle and Maui vegetable stir fry with ginger sesame broth. Your entrée can be complemented by a fine wine featured on the wine list chosen by Partner Chris Kiawe who stays current with new wines and interesting grapes and carefully selects the wines to match the food flavors.

Breakfast and lunch served from 8 a.m. to 3 p.m. daily: $6.00–14.00. Dinner nightly, entrées: $19.00–29.00. Reservations recommended. Visit The Plantation House on the web at theplantationhouse.com. And, try sister restaurants, The SeaWatch in Wailea (page134), and The Beach House on Kaua`i (page 20).

MEDITERRANEAN SAUTEED FISH WITH WILTED SPINACH

4 – 6 to 7 oz. pieces of fresh fish

½ pound spinach, cleaned and washed

5 Tbsp. olive oil

1 shallot, diced

2 tomatoes, diced

1 ½ Tbsp. Dijon mustard

1 oz. balsamic vinegar

juice of 1 lemon

2 Tbsp. calamata olives, pitted and diced

2 Tbsp. pine nuts

In a hot sauté pan, brown pine nuts for 2 minutes and remove; add 4 tablespoons olive oil and shallots, heat; add tomato, mustard, balsamic vinegar, lemon juice and olives. Toss to warm; add pine nuts and put into spinach that is in a bowl; toss to wilt.

In a hot sauté pan, put 1 tablespoon oil and roll around to coat pan. Cook fish 3 to 4 minutes on one side, seasoning with salt and pepper. Turn fish and finish cooking.

Divide wilted spinach onto 4 plates, top with fish and top fish with any tomato-pinenut mix that has fallen to the bottom of the bowl.

FISH WITH ASIAN MUSHROOM STIR FRY

4 – 6 to 7 oz. pieces of fresh fish

2 Tbsp. peanut oil

1 Tbsp. ginger, diced

1 Tbsp. garlic, diced

½ Maui onion, sliced paper thin

½ bunch green onions, diced whites, long greens

4 oz. shiitake mushrooms, stems off, sliced

4 oz. white mushrooms, sliced

2 Tbsp. oyster sauce

2 Tbsp. shoyu

2 Tbsp. water

2 Tbsp. butter

1 Tbsp. shichimi tagorashi

In a hot pan, put 1 tablespoon peanut oil; when oil is hot, add ginger and garlic, sauté 1 minute. Add onions and mushrooms, sauté until soft; add liquid, bring to a simmer and lower heat to low. In another hot sauté pan, add 1 tablespoon oil, swirl to coat pan. Dust fish with shichimi, salt and pepper, sauté 3 to 4 minutes, turn and finish for 4 to 5 minutes. While fish is finishing, bring mushrooms to a boil; add butter and reduce by half (approximately 4 to 5 minutes). Place fish on a plate with steamed rice and top with mushroom stew.

Serves 4.

$\mathcal{A}$ fun, lively and happening place, Sansei Seafood Restaurant & Sushi Bar hit the charts running and has continued to make a big splash in the culinary world every year since it opened in 1996. This friendly restaurant with out-standing food has been honored with many awards:1997 and 1998 Best Sushi Bar by *The Maui News* Readers Poll, 1998 and 1999 Highest Food Rating by *Zagat Survey* for Hawai`i Restaurants, 1998, 1999 and 2000 Hale `Aina Awards, and a 1999 Overall Rating of 90 from *Wine Spectator*, to name a few—an obvious sign that Sansei has all the right elements to continually please not only customers, but food critics as well.

Executive Chef/Owner D.K. Kodama is an "island boy" who travelled extensively, experiencing many different flavors and culinary styles, before returning to Hawai`i to share his wonderful expertise with us! He gives a lot of credit to his team, clocks in a tremendous amount of hours and when asked what pleases him, he says simply, "Dress casual, bring a smile, relax and enjoy the adventure of dining at Sansei."

Dining at Sansei is truly that—an adventure of flavors—creative and dreamy com-binations to tantalize your tongue. My favorites include the award-winning Mango Crab Salad Sushi Roll with Spicy Thai Vinaigrette and (also award-winning) Asian Rock Shrimp Cake with a Ginger-Lime Chili Butter and Cilantro Pesto. A great selection of sushi and fresh fish specials are featured and many other choices including Roasted Peking Duck Breast with foie gras demi glace. And this is the dessert that made me close my eyes and moan: Granny Smith Apple Tart with Caramel Sauce served warm with vanilla ice cream. It's sublime.

Open nightly. Sushi from $3.95, entrées from $15.95. Please call for reservations. Late night dining Thursday and Friday 10 p.m. to 1 a.m., with live karaoke entertainment. Be sure to visit the new Sansei at Restaurant Row on Oahu.

SANSEI SEAFOOD RESTAURANT & SUSHI BAR
(808) 669-6286 • The Shops at Kapalua, 115 Bay Drive, Unit 115, Kapalua, Maui 96761
(808) 536-6286 • Restaurant Row, 500 Ala Moana Blvd., Honolulu, O`ahu 96813

ASIAN ROCK SHRIMP CAKE
WITH GINGER LIME CHILI BUTTER AND CILANTRO PESTO
This Sansei original was voted "Best Appetizer" at "A Taste of Lahaina" 1996

SHRIMP CAKES

13 oz. raw rock shrimp (or other shrimp)

1 egg

1½ oz. mayonnaise

1 tsp. Dijon mustard

1 Tbsp. green onions, chopped

½ tsp. lemon juice

dash of Tabasco sauce

dash of black pepper

2 cups panko flakes

3 oz. bamboo shoots

Mix all ingredients together. Divide into ten equal portions and form cakes. Cover individual cakes with Chinese cake noodles or fresh angel hair pasta. Fry until golden brown.

GINGER LIME CHILI BUTTER

1 tsp. shallots, minced

¼ cup white wine

1 tsp. fresh ginger, chopped

juice of one lime

1 tsp. roux

3 oz. heavy whipping cream

¼ pound unsalted butter

¼ cup sweet Thai chili paste

salt to taste

Sauté shallots. Add wine, ginger and lime juice. Reduce by half. Add roux then add heavy cream. Reduce by half. Whip in butter. Strain and add Thai chili paste and mix.

CILANTRO PESTO

1 oz. macadamia nuts, chopped

1 oz. fresh cilantro, chopped

1 tsp. garlic, chopped

1 tsp. ginger, chopped

1 Tbsp. lime juice

½ cup virgin olive oil

dash salt

dash white pepper and shichimi*

Blend all ingredients together at high speed until smooth.

To assemble: Coat each appetizer-sized plate with the ginger lime chili butter. Dot with cilantro pesto. Sprinkle a garnish of shichimi. Top with two shrimp cakes. Enjoy! Serves 5.

*Japanese 7-spice pepper available at Asian grocery stores or in the Asian sections of the supermarket.

GRANNY SMITH APPLE TART WITH CARAMEL SAUCE

1 Granny Smith apple

3 puff pastry squares

1 egg

1 Tbsp. sugar

1 tsp. ground cinnamon

Cut apple into quarters and remove core. Slice the apple quarters thinly and set aside. Using a cookie cutter or coffee cup, press down on the puff pastry and cut into circles of approximately 5" in diameter. Using a fork, gently mark the puff pastry evenly. Beat the egg and brush onto the puff pastry. Place puff pastry on baking sheet lined with parchment paper. Arrange 12 to 16 apple slices in a circular pattern, overlapping slightly. Combine sugar and cinnamon; sprinkle mixture on top of apples. Bake in 400 degree oven for approx. 8 minutes or until golden brown.

CARAMEL SAUCE

4 cups sugar

2 cups water

1 quart heavy cream

1 pound unsalted butter

Melt sugar in water and caramelize until brown. Add heavy cream. Whip in butter. Stir until smooth.

To serve: Coat plate with warm caramel sauce. Place apple tart in the center of the plate. Serve with vanilla ice cream. Makes 3 individual tarts.

*W*ith sweeping views of green hills leading out to the vast expanse of blue ocean, Molokini, Kaho`olawe, and up to the ranch lands and cool air of Upcountry Maui, the SeaWatch Restaurant features a fresh cuisine that incorporates foods from all of these areas. Partner/Executive Chef Alex Purroy is inspired by this environment and says, "I like to cook good food with a conscience toward the culture." Inspired at an early age by his grandmother ("who was the best cook"), Chef Purroy is well traveled and includes

many ethnic influences in his approach. He recommends Grandma Purroy's Ciopinno with lobster, prawns and local fish; and the signature dish— fresh fish prepared Mauka style: tataki and peppered with sweet and sour Maui onions.

The SeaWatch interior is grand and comfortable with high ceilings, local artists' paintings and tropical foliage. Huge glass doors open to allow the magnificent view and fresh breezes inside, or you may enjoy dining outside under the vine-covered trellis on the lanai.

SeaWatch is open from 8 a.m. until 10 p.m. so you can enjoy a meal before or after your game of golf or a romantic sunset dinner.

Breakfast items include Crabcake Eggs Benedict with roasted pepper hollandaise, and French Toast. For lunch: Tropical Fish Quesadilla with fruit salsa; Mango Chutney Cashew Chicken Wrap; and a fresh catch.

Breakfast and lunch under $12.00. Dinner entrées: $20.00–29.00. Dinner reservations recommended. Look for SeaWatch on the web at seawatchrestaurant.com. And, try sister restaurants, The Plantation House in Kapalua (page 130), and The Beach House on Kaua`i (page 20).

DUCKLING LONG RICE WITH TRUFFLE OIL AND CALAMUNGI

1 roast duckling

6 cups carrots, sliced

6 cups onion, julienne

4 cups celery, bias cut

3 oz. garlic, minced

3 oz. ginger, minced

4 oz. sesame oil

1 cup shoyu (soy sauce)

2 packages long rice

1 cup calamungi leaves

4 oz. truffle oil

Remove meat from bones of the roasted duckling and shred. Make stock with bones and 1 gallon of water. Sauté carrots, onion, celery, garlic and ginger in sesame oil for 5 minutes. Strain duck stock into vegetables. Add long rice and calamungi. Simmer for 20 minutes. Finish by stirring in truffle oil and adjusting the seasonings with shoyu.

SPINY LOBSTER AND LEMONGRASS DIM SUM

12 oz. spiny lobster meat, chopped

1 oz. green onion

1 oz. cilantro

zest of 1 orange

1 Tbsp. ginger, minced

1 Tbsp. garlic, minced

1 Tbsp. sesame oil

salt and pepper to taste

24 wonton wrappers

24 lemongrass, cut in 3″ lengths

Mix all ingredients (except wonton wrappers and lemongrass) and place one ounce of mixture into wonton wrapper. Put end of lemongrass into center of wrapper and fold wonton up onto lemongrass stalk. Steam for approximately 8 minutes. Serve with your favorite dipping sauce.

STELLA BLUES CAFE

(808) 874-3779 • 1215 South Kihei Road. Kihei, Maui 96753

*W*henever I hear people recommend Stella Blues Café, they always explain, "They have *really good food*," and emphasize the last three words. In a town where many restaurants have a short life span, Janie and Ray Ennis are pleased that the community and visitors continue to frequent Stella Blues. Their goal, when they opened the restaurant, was to provide a fun, friendly place with affordable, high quality healthy food—and they have succeeded. The name comes from a Grateful Dead song and they usually have rock and roll music playing in the restaurant. You can also sit outside or get your food to go and enjoy a picnic at a beach nearby.

The menu offers a wide variety of items including some for children. For breakfast, try the South of the Border or the Banana Macadamia Nut Pancakes. (People love 'em!)

For lunch, they have great hearty salads: Cobb or Chicken Caesar; sandwiches: Stella's Special, spiced grilled eggplant, roasted garlic and sweet red peppers, feta cheese, cucumbers and greens with pesto mayo on homemade herb bread. This is a great flavorful sandwich. Fresh homemade soups change often and include Clam Chowder, Curry Chicken Veggie, Mexican Chicken and a variety of bean soups. Dinner features nightly specials of fresh fish and veggie items. The Thai Sweet Chili Chicken is a favorite, as is the Vegetarian Lasagna. Desserts can be enjoyed with a coffee drink; some of the supreme selections include: Vanilla and Chocolate Mousse Cake, Key Lime Pie and Chocolate Macadamia Nut Tart. Beer and wine are served featuring imports and microbrews, along with tropical drinks such as piña coladas and mango margaritas.

Open daily. Breakfast and lunch: $6.00–10.00.

Dinner: $11.00–19.00.

STELLA'S CLAM CHOWDER

½ pound baker potatoes, peeled and cubed

2 Tbsp. butter

1 large Maui onion, diced

½ gallon half and half

2 cups water

2 pounds diced canned clams

3 Tbsp. cornstarch

1½ tsp. salt

½ tsp. pepper

Boil potatoes until soft. In large pot, melt butter on medium-high, add onions and cook until translucent. Add cream, 1¾ cups water, potatoes and clams. Stir. Add cornstarch to remaining water, stir into paste and add to pot. Heat until slightly thick. Add salt and pepper. Serve warm.

MACADAMIA NUT CRUSTED ONO
WITH TROPICAL SALSA

1 large papaya

1 large mango

½ large pineapple

½ large white onion

1 Tbsp. white vinegar

¼ cup minced cilantro

1½ juiced limes

pinch of chili flake

2 large beaten eggs

2 cups macadamia nuts, chopped medium coarse

1½ pounds fresh ono fillets (6 oz. portions)

2–3 Tbsp. oil

Preheat oven to 350 degrees. Peel and dice papaya, mango, pineapple and onion. Place in mixing bowl. Add vinegar, cilantro, lime juice and chili flake. Mix and chill. Place eggs, flour and macadamia nuts in separate bowls. Lightly coat fillets with flour, dip in egg, then nuts. Place ono fillets in a lightly oiled shallow baking dish for 12–15 minutes until golden brown. Serve with salsa.

*W*hen you are a guest at The Ma'alaea Waterfront Restaurant, owners Donna, Gary and Rick Smith feel as though they are inviting you into their home and they want everything to be perfect. With a fabulous ocean-side location blended with exceptional service, incredibly fresh well-prepared fish and an intimate, romantic setting, it's no surprise that The Waterfront Restaurant has won numerous awards including "Best Seafood" and "Best Service" by *The Maui News* reader poll (for several consecutive years). Their outstanding wine list (which offers 27 wines by the glass!) has received the Award of Excellence from *Wine Spectator Magazine* for six years. This is sure sign of success, yet Gary explains, "It's nice to receive awards, but the real reward is the satisfaction we see in our guests' eyes and the fact that they return again and again. That's the best award we could ever receive."

Chef Bob Cambra likes to create food that is "good, hearty and rich, in a classical sort of way," and he wants guests to feel nourished and fulfilled after their meal. Five to eight fresh fish selections are available daily, offered with your choice of nine different preparations, such as Island Style with tiger prawns, sautéed scallions, carrots and shiitake mushrooms and a lemon grass, ginger and coconut milk jus lié; Hawaiian Salsa—broiled then topped with a Maui onion, fresh pineapple and three-pepper salsa. Lobster, chicken, steak, veal, lamb, tempting appetizers and a Lobster Chowder (to rave about!) are also offered. Entrées are served with fresh-baked Maui onion bread and homemade Hawaiian beer cheese, fresh vegetables and herbed rice or selected potatoes. Be sure to save room for dessert.

Open nightly. Dinner from $17.95. Call for reservations. Visit their web site at waterfrontrestaurant.net.

SAUTEED HAWAIIAN SEA BASS WITH MARINATED PRAWNS AND COCONUT, LEMON GRASS & GINGER CREAM

4 – 6 oz. pieces Hawaiian sea bass (hapu`u)
8 pieces 16/20 prawns
½ pound shiitake mushrooms, sliced
1 head bok choy, chopped
4 oz. green onions, chopped
1 medium carrot, julienne

Marinade ingredients:
½ cup sugar
½ cup shoyu (soy sauce)
⅛ cup rice vinegar
2 Tbsp. sherry wine
2 Tbsp. sesame oil
1 Tbsp. ginger, minced
1 tsp. garlic, minced

Mix all marinade ingredients together. Marinate prawns for a half hour. Sauté prawns and vegetables and serve with Coconut, Lemon Grass & Ginger Cream.

COCONUT, LEMON GRASS & GINGER CREAM

1 cup onion, chopped
2 Tbsp. Szchewan peppercorns
2 Tbsp. ginger, minced
1 stalk lemon grass, chopped
2 Tbsp. whole unsalted butter
3 oz. white wine
1 pint heavy cream

1 cup coconut milk
½ cup chicken stock
½ cup clam stock
⅛ cup white sugar
1 tsp. Vietnamese chili paste
⅛ cup cilantro, chopped
corn starch to thicken

Sweat onions, peppercorns, ginger and lemon grass in butter. Add white wine, heavy cream, coconut milk, and both chicken and clam stocks. Bring to a boil and finish with Vietnamese chili paste and cilantro. Simmer for 10 minutes and thicken with 1 tablespoon of cornstarch and water mixture. Strain sauce before serving. Yields 4 servings.

FRESH BLUEBERRY WHITE CHOCOLATE CHEESECAKE

2 cups white chocolate chips
2 cups heavy cream
3 pounds cream cheese
¾ cup white sugar

6 whole eggs
1 tsp. vanilla
2 cups fresh blueberries

Melt chocolate and 1 cup of the heavy cream in microwave for 1½ minutes. Cream cheese in mixer with paddle. In separate mixing bowl, whip eggs and vanilla. Add sugar and heavy cream to cream cheese; mix for 5 minutes. Add melted chocolate and mix until incorporated; then add egg and vanilla mixture and whip until blended. Alternate cream cheese mixture and blueberries in Chocolate Macadamia Nut Crust lined spring form pan. Finish with blueberries on top. Bake at 300 degrees for 2 hours. Cool 6 hours before serving.

CHOCOLATE MACADAMIA NUT CRUST

8 oz. unsalted butter
1 cup graham cracker crumbs
½ cup sugar

1½ cups macadamia nuts, diced
¼ cup cocoa powder

Melt butter in microwave. In mixer, combine all dry ingredients until well mixed. Add butter and mix well. Form crust in spring form pan. Refrigerate until ready to use.

Lana`i

The Pineapple Island

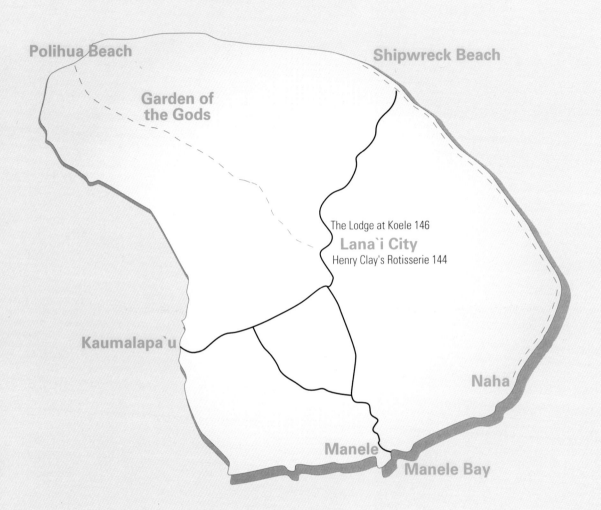

Polihua Beach

Shipwreck Beach

Garden of
the Gods

The Lodge at Koele 146
Lana`i City
Henry Clay's Rotisserie 144

Kaumalapa`u

Naha

Manele

Manele Bay

Lana`i

Restaurant, Type of Cuisine,
Recipes Featured

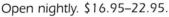

The charm, character and hearty "soul food" of **Henry Clay's Rotisserie** makes it a unique complement to the resort restaurants on the quiet island of Lana'i. Popular with local residents and visitors alike, Henry Clay's is located in the Hotel Lana'i, which was originally built in 1923 by James Dole to accommodate and entertain visiting pineapple executives. Beautifully remodeled, the restaurant is warm and cozy with hardwood floors, watercolors by local artists, an exhibition kitchen and a brick fireplace for chilly evenings. (They're at 2,000 feet elevation.) And, if you'd like to experience the contrast of cool crisp air with warm food, try dining in the peaceful patio under a grove of towering Norfolk pines.

Chef/Owner Henry Clay Richardson, originally from French Louisiana, is a family man and creates a feeling of family in his restaurant where you will be served generous portions of food that he likes to "keep as simple and fresh as possible; keeping it fun." Rajun Cajun Clay's Shrimp is "to die for" and "extremely habit forming." If you can stop eating the incredible shrimp, you'll have room for Louisiana Style Baby Back Ribs, down home "Barbeque" cajun seasoned and rotisserie fired; Lana'i's fresh catch of the day; Rotisserie Roasted Chicken, or a Gourmet Pizza. When the mood is right, you may even hear an impromptu horn performance by Henry Clay Richardson, Sr. Even his son doesn't know when he will delight diners with jazz, blues and R&B standards until the sweet sounds of the horn come wafting into the kitchen.

Open nightly. $16.95–22.95.

RAJUN CAJUN CLAY'S SHRIMP

"This recipe is inspired by the robust combinations of flavors that are in New Orleans. Feel free to experiment with ingredients to create your own taste. If you like spice, add more. If butter is a concern, use extra virgin olive oil instead. Try the sauce with any seafood or fish. Enjoy!"

8 gulf shrimp, peeled and deveined
Cajun seasoning to taste
1 oz. olive oil
½ tsp. garlic, minced
½ tsp. shallots, diced fine
½ tsp. mixed herbs (thyme, chervil, rosemary, Italian parsley, oregano)
½ tsp. Cajun seasoning mix

1 tsp. scallions, chopped
⅛ tsp. white pepper, fresh ground
½ tsp. black pepper, fresh ground
½ tsp. fresh lemon juice
1 anchovy fillet, chop to make paste (or substitute Worcestershire sauce)
2 oz. seafood, fish stock or clam juice
1 ½ Tbsp. unsalted butter, room temperature

Season the shrimp with the Cajun seasoning, sauté over medium heat (high heat will burn the spices). Cook until half done; add herbs and continue to sauté to "aroma." Add lemon juice and anchovy paste; pour in seafood stock and reduce until only ¼ of the stock remains. Whip the butter in to create consistency of the sauce. Do not boil, as this will cause the sauce to "break."

"This is a fast recipe to cook, once all the ingredients are assembled. By the time the sauce is completed, the shrimp should be cooked just right. I mix my own Cajun seasoning. Store mixes usually contain too much salt, so reduce the amount used in this recipe." —Henry Clay

FAMOUS PECAN PIE

10 oz. light brown sugar
6 extra large eggs
2 egg yolks
16 oz. light Karo syrup
2 tsp. dark creme de cocoa

2 tsp. vanilla extract
1 pinch ground cinnamon
2 oz. unsalted butter, melted
2 – 10" pie dough shells
10 oz. chopped pecans

Place sugar and eggs in mixing bowl, whip to combine. Do not incorporate too much air. Stir in all remaining ingredients, except pecans. Divide pecans evenly into 2 pie shells and pour equal amounts of batter over them. Gently mix pecans into batter to coat. Bake at 325 degrees for 1¼ to 1½ hours until done. Allow to cool for at least one hour before serving.

PIE DOUGH

10 oz. unsalted butter, COLD
1 pinch salt

16 oz. all purpose flour
½ cup water, ICE COLD

Place all ingredients into mixing bowl, excluding the water. With your hands, "massage" the mixture until the butter is about the size of a pea; do not allow to become too soft. Place bowl onto mixer with paddle attachment. On low speed, add the water, mix until a dough ball is formed. Remove dough from bowl and place on a table dusted with flour. Mold into an even cylinder shape. Do not over knead. Cover with food wrap; rest in refrigerator for approximately 15 minutes, then divide into 2 equal parts and roll out to fit 10 inch pans. Shape edges and place in refrigerator to stiffen before use.

"This recipe has been enjoyed by my guests in Hawai`i since 1982. I believe that the slow, low temperature cooking is the key. Enjoy with homemade ice cream and cafe au lait." —Henry Clay

*S*erene and beautiful, The Lodge at Koele offers refinement and grace on the quiet island of Lana`i. It is a place where kama`ainas (Hawai`i residents) go to get away, and travelers from all over the world are seduced by the special qualities of this relaxed, scenic paradise set in the central uplands of Lana`i.

Recognized by *Condé Nast Traveler*, *Zagat*, *Gourmet* and *Bon Appétit* magazines, among others, the Lodge continually receives awards and top ratings. It is wonderful to experience the blend of warm aloha from the long-time local residents, who make up most of the staff, with the inviting elegance of a top resort.

The Lodge at Koele offers two dining choices: The Formal Dining Room, warmed by the glow of the fireplace, and the Terrace Restaurant, which is open to the Great Hall where live piano can be heard in the evenings and views of the pristine gardens can be seen during the day. For guests of the Lodge, a traditional afternoon tea is presented in the Music Room.

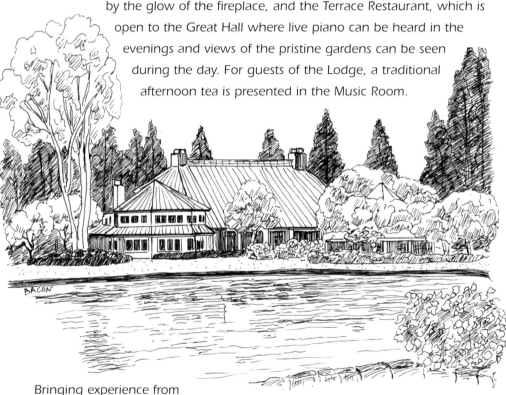

Bringing experience from top resorts around the world, Executive Chef Andrew Manion-Copley creates what he likes to call "Hawaiian Country" cuisine. Seasonal menus reflect the subtle changes in climate and fit the natural environment utilizing produce, fish and even meats from the island including: Roasted Lana`i Venison Loin rolled in cracked black pepper with layered sweet potatoes and pineapple cider sauce. The fresh catch I enjoyed was Grilled Opah with spinach shrimp risotto, caramelized Maui onions. The flavors were light and fresh; the presentation elegant.

The Terrace Restaurant serves breakfast, lunch and dinner. Dinner entrées: $17.00–27.00. The Formal Dining Room serves dinner only; entrées begin at $38.00. Jacket required.

CRISPY SKIN HAWAIIAN MOI ON BRAISED WHITE BEANS WITH FRESH CLAMS AND FOREST MUSHROOMS

For the beans:
½ cup dried white beans, soaked overnight
1 medium carrot, diced
1 medium onion, diced
1 medium celery, diced
2 sprigs fresh parsley
1 branch fresh rosemary
1 sage leaf
4 cups chicken stock

For the forest mushrooms:
1 cup chanterelles
½ cup oyster mushrooms
1 lemon skin, finely diced

5 basil leaves, chopped
2 Tbsp. olive oil
1 Tbsp. butter

For the moi and clams:
4 fillets fresh moi
16 fresh clams
1 Tbsp. olive oil
1 small shallot, finely chopped
1 medium garlic clove, finely chopped
4 cups fish stock
1 cup dry white wine
2 Tbsp. butter
1 Tbsp. olive oil

Sauté carrot, onion, celery, parsley and rosemary in oil for 3 minutes. Add sage and white beans; cover with chicken stock. Simmer for about 1½ hours.

To prepare the mushrooms: Melt butter and oil in a pan; add both mushrooms, lemon skin and basil. Sauté until mushrooms are soft and golden brown. Add lemon juice and season.

In hot oil, sauté moi until cooked, set aside and keep warm. In the same pan, add shallots and garlic; sauté for 2 minutes. Add clams, sauté another 2 minutes. Deglaze with wine; add fish stock and simmer until clams open. Set aside and keep warm. Reduce the cooking liquor by half. Mix the beans and mushrooms together and sauté in a hot pan, place the mixture in the center of the plate with the fish on top and the clams around. Add the butter to cooking liquor; whisk, season and pour over the clams.

Hawai`i

The Big Island

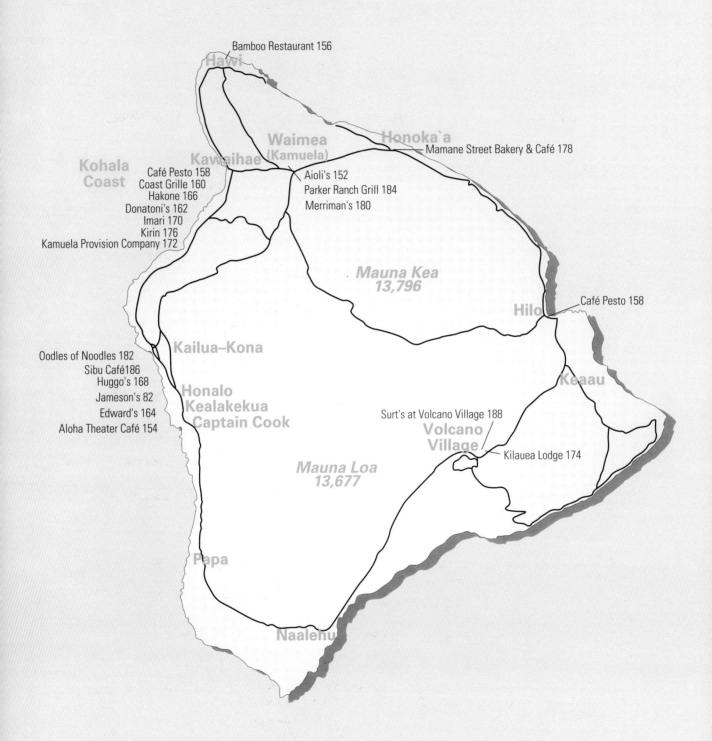

Bamboo Restaurant 156

Hawi

Waimea
(Kamuela)

Honoka`a

Mamane Street Bakery & Café 178

Kawaihae

Kohala
Coast

Café Pesto 158
Coast Grille 160
Hakone 166
Donatoni's 162
Imari 170
Kirin 176
Kamuela Provision Company 172

Aioli's 152
Parker Ranch Grill 184
Merriman's 180

Mauna Kea
13,796

Hilo

Café Pesto 158

Oodles of Noodles 182
Sibu Café186
Huggo's 168
Jameson's 82
Edward's 164
Aloha Theater Café 154

Kailua–Kona

Keaau

Honalo
Kealakekua
Captain Cook

Surt's at Volcano Village 188

Volcano
Village

Kilauea Lodge 174

Mauna Loa
13,677

Papa

Naalehu

Hawai`i

Restaurant, Page, Type of Cuisine
Recipes Featured

A little serendipity occurred when owner/chef Jerry Mills and co-owner/ manager Stephen Hall chose the name **Aioli's**. They chose it because they like to cook with garlic; it's early in the alphabet and sounds Hawaiian. Only later did they find out from a customer that it means "joyful food" or "joyful sex" in Hawaiian (depending on whether there is an okina placed in front of the first a — `aioli means joyful food). Jerry and Stephen have created a unique little gem where, as Jerry says, they offer "food that is attractive, but not pretentious." Aioli's is small, comfortable and friendly. The tables are covered with paper; crayons are offered for artistic expression, some of which is later displayed in the restaurant and then sold for charity.

Lunch features homemade soups (the Garlic Soup is a specialty), salads and sandwiches. I had the fresh catch on some of their homemade bread, which was delicious and comes with tasty seasoned waffle-type fries. As I was finishing my sandwich, I watched their homemade cookies quickly disappearing to eager customers, so I had to try them too, and they're great.

Aioli's changes their dinner menu every two weeks, offering items such as fresh local fish, and Venison Tournedos with Pomegranate Sauce served with local corn and garlicky mashed potatoes. A couple of vegetarian dishes are always featured. Examples are: Spinach Mushroom Lasagna with garlic bread, or Vegetable Stir-Fry with Coconut-Basil Sauce. For dessert, the Lilikoi Cheesecake is outrageous—lusciously creamy with a perfect flavorful tang. Aioli's allows you to bring your own bottle of wine. If you drop it by early, they'll keep it chilled for you, and there's no corkage fee.

Lunch under $10.00. Dinner entrées: $11.95–20.95. Open 11 a.m. to 8 p.m. Tuesday through Thursday; until 9 p.m. Friday and Saturday, and 8 a.m. to 2 p.m. on Sundays. Located behind Merriman's.

MAHIMAHI IN "EDIBLE PARCHMENT" WITH ASIAN PACIFIC SAUCE

8 pieces of thinly sliced mahimahi fillets (2 to 2½ oz. each)

8 large spinach leaves (or equal amount of smaller leaves)

1 Tbsp. garlic, crushed

8 spring roll wrappers, approx. 8½" diameter, dried type*

1 Tbsp. olive or vegetable oil

Dip the spring roll wrappers (one or two at a time) in warm water for a few seconds. Drain the wrappers and lay them flat on a counter top or cutting board and allow them to set for 1 to 2 minutes until they are completely flexible. Lay a spinach leaf, smeared with a small amount of crushed garlic, on the wrapper about 2" from the edge. Place a fillet of mahimahi on top of the spinach leaf and fold the near side of the wrapper over the fish. Then fold the right and left sides of the wrapper and finally wrap the far side over the fish, encasing the mahimahi and spinach in a spring roll wrap. Repeat the process with the remaining 7 pieces of fish.
In a large skillet (or 2 smaller ones), heat the oil to medium hot and place 4 wraps in the skillet. Do not crowd the fish packets. Sauté for about 2 minutes, then flip the wraps over and cook about 2 more minutes. The spring roll wrappers should be firm and slightly browned. Remove the packets and place on a plate. Quickly repeat the cooking process with the remaining fish. Drizzle about a tablespoon of sauce on top of each packet and serve immediately. Serving size: 2 packets.
*Available in Asian markets and the Asian section of most grocery stores.

ASIAN PACIFIC SAUCE

The garlic chives in this sauce yield an essential complexity. It is best to make the sauce at least an hour before using.

½ cup soy (shoyu) sauce, preferably Kikkoman

¼ tsp. fresh ginger, grated

1 Tbsp. garlic, crushed

2 tsp. sesame oil

1 Tbsp. fresh snipped garlic chives

Blend all ingredients together. Drizzle about one tablespoon over each fish packet.

BAKED GARLIC CLOVES WITH BRIE AND WALNUTS IN PHYLLO

16 garlic cloves, large size, cleaned

1 Tbsp. olive oil

4 phyllo sheets

½ cup butter, melted

16 walnut halves

16 tsp. brie

Toss the garlic cloves with oil; then place garlic in a single layer on aluminum foil. Fold and seal sides, keeping garlic in a single layer. Place package on a cookie sheet and bake in a preheated 350 degree oven for 30 minutes. When done, open foil and allow garlic to cool.

Place a sheet of phyllo dough on flat surface with long side of sheet parallel to you. Brush melted butter lightly over entire surface. With a sharp knife, gently cut the sheet towards you into four equal strips. At the top of a strip, place a walnut half, topped with 1 teaspoon brie and a baked garlic clove. Fold about ½" of each long side of the strip over, partially covering the walnut assembly. Lightly butter the strip. Fold the phyllo around the walnut/brie/garlic into a triangle or cylinder shape. Brush the finished wrap again with butter. Repeat the process with the remaining walnut/brie/garlic combinations. At this point, the appetizers can be refrigerated for 1 to 2 days before cooking.

Preheat oven to 375 degrees. Bake for 20–25 minutes until puffed and golden.
Serving size: 2 pieces.

*C*heerful, comfortable and artsy, the **Aloha Theatre Café** is an all-time favorite you won't want to miss. They have been featured in *Food and Wine*, *Bon Appétit*, and *Gourmet Magazine*. *Hidden Hawaii*, *Frommer's* and *Zagat Survey* gave the Aloha Café top ratings.

The Aloha Café is located in the historic Aloha Theatre building, which was built in 1932. You can dine inside where local art is displayed or sit outside on the long narrow lanai where fresh breezes and sweeping views of pastureland lead out to the ocean.

The theatre actively shows art and independent films, as well as hosting live performances featuring dance, music and theater. (Call 322-2323 for information.) The Aloha Store, which is also located in the complex, features fine handmade crafts by island artists including jewelry, clothing, books, and toys.

Breakfast at the Café includes delicious pancakes, fresh fruit, homemade muffins, fluffy omelets and tofu scrambles. Lunch features unique homemade soups and fresh baked breads, thick sandwiches, great hamburgers, vegetarian specials and the "freshest" fish daily. The dinner menu, focused around Theatre nights, shows a new flair for fresh island cuisine that has received rave reviews. The Aloha Café will tempt you with outstanding homemade desserts: pies, cakes, tortes, cookies, biscottis and other lustful goodies. Espresso drinks, 100% pure Kona coffee, imported and domestic beers and wines are also offered.

Open daily 8 a.m. until 3 p.m. Breakfast and lunch average $7.00. Dinner: $8.00–17.00, served Thursday, Friday and Saturday until 9 p.m. The Aloha Café is located just 10 miles south of Kailua-Kona.

TARO CRUSTED `AHI WITH LEHUA HONEY-LIME TARTAR

4 fresh `ahi fillets, 6 oz. each
8 oz. taro chips
¼ cup flour
1 egg

½ cup water
salt and pepper to taste
2 Tbsp. olive oil

Make the Lehua Honey-Lime Tartar. Then place taro chips in food processor and chop to fine consistency. Set crumbs aside. Mix beaten egg with water. Salt and pepper the fillets, dust in flour, dip in egg wash. Press each `ahi fillet firmly into taro crumbs. Sauté `ahi in olive oil over medium heat for 1 minute on each side. Then bake at 350 degrees for 10 minutes. Serve tartar with fish.

Makes 4 servings.

Recipe by Chef Dennies De La Cruz

LEHUA HONEY-LIME TARTAR

⅛ cup fresh lime juice
1 cup mayonnaise
2 Tbsp. pickle relish

¼ cup lehua honey
salt and white pepper to taste

Mix all ingredients and set aside.

ALOHA THEATER LILIKOI BARS

SHORTBREAD CRUST

1½ cups butter
1 cup sugar

3 cups flour

Cream butter and sugar. Add flour. Press evenly into greased 9x13" pan and build up the sides.

LILIKOI MIX

4 eggs
1¾ cups sugar
½ cup lilikoi juice
1 tsp. baking powder

½ cup flour
pinch of salt
powdered sugar

Beat eggs, add sugar gradually, then add lilikoi juice. Sift flour, baking powder and salt together. Add dry ingredients to liquid mixture. Filling will be watery. Pour over crust and bake in preheated 350 degree oven for 35–40 minutes until firm to the touch. Sprinkle with powdered sugar.

Recipe by Baker Cathy Haber.

𝓤nique and inviting, **Bamboo Restaurant** gives the feeling of stepping back in time. You will undoubtedly enjoy experiencing a bit of Old Hawai'i, complete with lots of aloha and friendly Hawaiian "aunties" who will graciously charm and entertain you, and if you're lucky, maybe even break into an impromptu hula. Bamboo is located in a restored historic Hawaiian building that is filled with tropical flowers and plants, bamboo accents and old Hawai'i memorabilia. It's a fun and lively gathering place for the community and a *must* experience for the visitor.

Featuring fresh fish, organic herbs from their garden and produce from local farmers, Bamboo offers delightful food like Hawai'i Thai fish on a bed of green papaya salad, topped with warm coconut sauce, garnished with fresh bean sprouts, cilantro, roasted peanuts and green onions, Chicken Saté Pot Stickers, Margarita Prawns and some tasty vegetarian items. Rumor has it that they invented Passion Fruit (lilikoi) Margaritas that could jazz up your night along with the live Hawaiian entertainment on Friday and Saturday evenings.

Since Bamboo opened in 1993, the historical town of Hawi (birthplace of King Kamehameha) has been restored and now has many quaint shops, a center for the arts, and eco-tourism—kayaking, hiking, horseback riding and more. It's definitely worth the drive to Hawi! Be sure to check out the Kohala Koa Gallery at Bamboo featuring fine Koa wood furniture, art and hand crafted items.

Open Tuesday through Saturday for lunch ($6.00–10.00) and dinner ($8.00–20.00) and Sunday brunch ($5.00-10.00). They are closed Mondays. Dinner reservations requested.

CHICKEN SATE POT STICKERS
FILLING

1 pound ground chicken

2 Tbsp. garlic, minced

2 Tbsp. fresh ginger, minced

2 Tbsp. shallots, minced

Sauté together until the chicken is thoroughly cooked. Drain off the excess fat and then mix the chicken together in a bowl with:

1 cup chunky peanut butter

¼ cup brown sugar

2 Tbsp. Thai hot chili paste

2 Tbsp. fresh basil, chopped

2 Tbsp. fresh cilantro, chopped

Chill the mixture, and then wrap in won ton wrappers. Bring the edges into a corner or simply fold into triangles, using a dab of water to "glue" the edges. Find the shape that is best for you! Steam the pot stickers for 8–10 minutes, until the wrappers are translucent, and serve with Chili Mint Dipping Sauce.

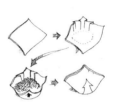

CHILI MINT SAUCE

1 small bottle of Thai sweet chili sauce

¼ cup rice wine vinegar

½ cup sugar

¼ cup cilantro, chopped

¼ cup fresh mint, chopped

1 tsp. sesame oil

Purée ingredients in a food processor for 1 minute. Serve at room temperature.

MARGARITA PRAWNS

3 to 4 large prawns per person

Butterfly the prawns, leaving tail on. Grill or sauté lightly in a pan with butter and lime juice. Pour warm Margarita Sauce on a plate and arrange prawns in the sauce. Garnish with fresh papaya salsa or tropical fresh fruit salsa and sprigs of fresh cilantro.

MARGARITA SAUCE

1 Tbsp. butter

1½ Tbsp. garlic

1 Tbsp. sambal

1 oz. tequila

juice of one juicy lime

1½ cups heavy cream

½ Tbsp. cornstarch mixed with 2 Tbsp. water

salt and pepper to taste

Lightly sauté garlic and sambal with butter. Add tequila and flame off the alcohol. Add lime juice and heavy cream; bring to a light boil and reduce slightly. Thicken with cornstarch and season with salt and pepper.

CAFE PESTO

(808) 969-6640 • 308 Kamehameha Avenue, Hilo, Hawai'i 96720

(808) 882-1071 • Kawaihae Shopping Center, Hwy. 270, Kawaihae, S. Kohala Coast, Hawai'i 96743

*S*ince the first edition of *Tasting Paradise*, **Café Pesto** has continued to grow in popularity and notability. With their bold black and white checkered floors and the classic red rose on each table, they have captured the right combination of a chic upbeat contemporary atmosphere and outstanding creative island cuisine. Some of the awards they've won include: "Hawai'i Top Restaurants," 1996–1999 *Zagat Survey Restaurant Guide*; "Best Big Island Restaurant,"1999 and 2000 *Honolulu Magazine* Hale 'Aina Awards; and "Best of Hawai'i's Hidden Treasures," *Fodor's Travel Guide*.

Café Pesto's menu is diverse, fresh and intriguing, including their delicious Asian Pacific Crab Cakes with honey-miso vinaigrette; an outrageous pizza with Chili Grilled Shrimp, shiitake mushrooms, green onions and cilantro créme fraiche. Also fresh seafood, distinctive salads,

and amazing desserts that you can enjoy with an espresso or cappuccino complete the menu.

Casual and fun, Café Pesto stays open all afternoon through dinner—so you don't have to wait to titillate your taste buds.

Café Pesto, Hilo Bay is located in the renovated S. Hata Building in historic downtown Hilo, and on the ocean side of the Kawaihae Shopping Center. Lunch: $8.00–12.00. Dinner: $14.00–23.00. Open daily. Find them on the web: cafepesto.com.

CRABCAKES WITH HONEY-MISO VINAIGRETTE

¼ cup Maui onion, diced small
¼ cup celery, diced small
2 Tbsp. red bell pepper, diced small
2 Tbsp. yellow bell pepper, diced small
¾ cup crab meat, squeezed dry, inspect for shells
¼ cup mayonnaise

¼ cup panko flakes
1 tsp. roasted garlic, minced
1 Tbsp. Dijon mustard
1 Tbsp. sweet chili sauce
For breading: flour, egg and panko

Sauté diced onion, celery and peppers. Cool down. Combine all ingredients. Test for seasoning. Using a small scooper, portion out crabcakes. They should weigh 1½ ounces before breading. Bread crabcakes using standard breading procedure: Dip crabcake balls into flour, egg, then panko. Flatten into patties. Set on a tray lined with parchment paper. Chill until ready to serve. Cook in 350 degree vegetable oil until golden brown. Drain finished crabcakes on a clean paper towel to remove all excess oil.

HONEY-MISO VINAIGRETTE

1 Tbsp. pickled ginger, white
½ tsp. garlic, minced
½ cup honey
½ cup rice vinegar

½ tsp. sugar
1 egg yolk
2 Tbsp. miso paste
1½ cups oil, preferably canola

Place all ingredients (except oil) in a blender. Turn blender on low at first, then on high. Add peanut oil slowly while blender is running. Once well incorporated, turn blender off. Pour into appropriate storage container.

COAST GRILLE

(808) 880-3011 • Hapuna Beach Prince Hotel, Kamuela, Hawai'i 96743

*D*ining al fresco on the lanai with tropical breezes and the soft sound of the surf accented by fuchsia Bougainvillea and palm trees, Coast Grille is the perfect place to enjoy a romantic sunset dinner with a quintessential Hawaiian sunset view.

This fabulous restaurant is a 1999 Hale `Aina Award winner and it's easy to see why— Coast Grille provides an exquisite dining experience from the setting to the service and the phenomenal food. The striking grand architecture is reminiscent of a Frank Lloyd Wright design with large columns and a high circular ceiling, high windows and a Hawaiian flair—colorful fish painted near the ceiling and large tropical bouquets and plants. There is also an impressive marble bar and a marble oyster bar where a variety of exceptionally fresh oysters are served. The restaurant is open air and with three tiers of seating; it offers almost every table a view of beautiful Hapuna beach.

Coast Grille presents an exceptional menu with chef's specials featured daily. The Crispy Crab Cakes are a great appetizer—pleasing to both the palette and the eye, and Kona Lobster Sushi (recipe at right) is unique and remarkably delicious. We tried the Chef's Selection of Fresh Hawaiian Fish and enjoyed sampling three superb combinations, Sautéed Ono with lemon Miso cream sauce, Blackened Mahimahi with Asian pear chutney, and Peppery `Ahi with Mango vinaigrette. (These combinations change daily.) Coast Grille has its own herb garden, and they feature an extensive wine list with an outstanding champagne selection. And the desserts . . . a hard choice, we finally decided on the Kona Cheesecake with Mocha Sauce and Lemon Whip Cream. Yum!

Dinner served nightly. Entrées: $23.00-36.00. Please call for reservations.

FURIKAKE CRUSTED SWORDFISH STEAK

4 swordfish steaks, 6 oz. each
4 tsp. furikake
8 oz. baby bok choy
12 taro ravioli

8 Tbsp. rock shrimp mushroom ragout
8 Tbsp. Ka'u orange butter sauce
12 Ka'u (or other) orange segments
salt and pepper to taste

Prepare Ravioli, Rock Shrimp Mushroom Ragout and Orange Butter Sauce. Then season the swordfish with salt and pepper. To one side of the swordfish, add furikake (not too much); just enough for a light coat. In a medium sauté pan, heat oil and sauté swordfish with the furikake crust side down first. You can finish this in the oven if you prefer. When finished, let rest for a minute. Cook the baby bok choy and arrange on plate. To re-heat the ravioli, you can either heat them in boiling water or a Chinese steamer.

TARO RAVIOLI

8 oz. taro, peeled and diced
4 Tbsp. Maui onion, diced
2 tsp. ginger, chopped
2 tsp. garlic, chopped
¼ cup coconut milk

4 tsp. lemon juice
2 tsp. yellow curry paste
¼ cup butter
16 large round won ton wrappers

Steam taro for 45 minutes. In sauce pot, caramelize Maui onion, ginger and garlic in the butter. Then add coconut milk, curry paste and lemon juice. Bring to a boil. Then add to steamed taro in mixing bowl and mix with paddle until smooth. Divide the taro mixture into 16 equal amounts on the won ton wrappers. Cook ravioli in boiling water until al dente. Hold until needed.

ROCK SHRIMP MUSHROOM RAGOUT

8 oz. rock shrimp
½ cup tomato, diced and de-seeded
½ cup cucumber, peeled, diced and de-seeded
¼ cup water chestnuts, diced
¼ cup mirin

4 oz. shiitake mushroom, diced
¼ cup cilantro
¼ cup green onions
¼ cup salad oil
salt and pepper to taste

Season the rock shrimp and sauté until cooked, in a non-stick pan with a touch of oil. Let cool. In a small bowl, add tomato, cucumber, water chestnuts and rock shrimp, mushroom, cilantro, and green onions. Season with mirin, salad oil, salt and pepper.

KA'U ORANGE BUTTER SAUCE

4 Tbsp. shallots, minced
12 pieces of white peppercorn
2 bay leaves
2 cups white wine

4 Ka'u (or other type) oranges, juice from
2¼ cups butter, unsalted, at room
    temperature

In a small pot, sweat out the shallots until translucent. Add peppercorn, bay leaves, wine and orange juice. Slowly fold in the butter until all is incorporated. Season. Strain through a fine chinos.

Executive Chef Corey A. Waite

*R*ich and welcoming, Donatoni's is like an Italian villa with intimate rooms, an elegant decor including chandeliers and fine paintings, large comfortable chairs, and, with a little imagination, the boats drifting by on the lagoon just a step off the terrace could be gondolas. It is where Hawai'i blends with Italy. The outdoor terrace offers a romantic setting to watch the stars appear while enjoying a bottle of fine wine from their extensive selection. And, if you like to keep up with the celebrity stars, notice the photos of Tom Cruise and Nicole Kidman, Clint Eastwood, Billy Crystal and others who have dined at Donatoni's.

The chef at Donatoni's brings authentic Italian food to Hawai'i, utilizing fresh local produce. Specialties include the fresh catch of the day, and Ciopinno from an authentic Italian recipe made with local fish. We started with the Crostatina Di Salmone E Rucola—smoked salmon on pizzette with shallots, capers and arugula, which is a great choice for an appetizer. I had the fresh catch of the day for my entrée: Swordfish with asparagus and risotto with a sublime light creamy sauce and caramelized Maui onions. I couldn't help but close my eyes and try not to moan too loudly each time I took a bite. It was melt-in-your-mouth perfection. For dessert: Torta di Albicocche, light apricot mousse, roasted apricots and lemon cream in Italian meringue, and Torta di Cioccolato e Noci, Hawaiian vintage chocolate caramel mousse with crunchy walnut cougatine. They were so smooth and dreamy; we ate every last bite. Amazing.

Dinner only. Entrées: $19.00–32.00. Call for reservations and nights open.

OSSOBUCO IN CREMOLATA

6 – 14 to 16 oz. veal shanks

6 oz. flour

¼ cup olive oil

4 oz. butter

2 scams rosemary

10 leaves sage

1.2 oz. each carrots, celery, and onions

1 cup white wine

¾ cup tomato sauce

¾ cup demi or brown gravy

lemon zest from 2 lemons

20 oz. risotto or mashed potatoes

Flour the veal shanks on both sides, then sear in hot olive oil, butter, rosemary and sage until almost brown in color. Discard the cooking oil and replace with fresh oil. Mince the vegetables very fine. Sauté the ossobuco with the vegetables. Add white wine and let reduce by half, then add tomato sauce and demi (or brown gravy). Cover with foil and bake in preheated oven at 350 degrees for about 1 hour until meat is tender but not mushy. Strain the sauce. Put the ossobuco on the risotto or mashed potatoes nestled with the sauce and lemon zest on top.

Serves 6.

SELLA D'AGNELLO IN CROSTA DI PISTACCHIO

6 racks of lamb

6 Tbsp. olive oil

4 oz. butter

3 scams rosemary

6 cloves garlic, minced

6 Tbsp. Dijon mustard

8 oz. seasoned bread crumbs

3 oz. pistachio nuts, crushed

4 shallots, chopped

6 to 8 stems thyme

1½ cups red wine (Cabernet)

1 cup demi or brown gravy

6 cooked pears

12 oz. mashed potatoes

salt and pepper to taste

Sear the racks on front and back side very well in hot olive oil and butter with rosemary, garlic, salt and pepper, giving a nice brown color. Spread the mustard on the lamb rack; dust with seasoned bread crumbs and crushed pistachio nuts. Bake in preheated oven at 350 degrees, until done. While baking, make the sauce: Braise the chopped shallots with fresh thyme in a tablespoon of hot olive oil until becomes golden; add the red wine and let reduce by half, add demi or brown gravy. Reduce the sauce consistency and strain. Slice each rack of lamb in 6 chops. Lay on the mashed potatoes and place the precooked pear close to the lamb. Top with sauce.

Serves 6.

Chef Sascia Marchesi

As the sun sets into the glistening ocean, tiki torches create a soft romantic glow in the intimate, elemental setting of Edward's. Less than twenty tables share the covered terrace just steps from crashing ocean waves.

Chef and owner Edward Frady, who was honored as the 1999 Western Regional Chef of the Year, serves sensational Mediterranean cuisine such as Fresh Salmon and Shrimp Agean—sautéed salmon and shrimp on a sauce of roasted red pepper purée with shallots, mushroom and artichokes with herb angel hair pasta, or a seasonal fresh fish with choice of sauce. Greek Pastichio (Greek Pasta Pie) and salad is an example of a daily special. For lunch, try the Salad Niçoise, a mixture of greens, tomato, boiled eggs, green beans, French potato salad, and topped with fresh grilled tuna. Breakfast features Eggs Benedict or Banana Macadamia Nut Waffle with an apple spice sausage patty.

Island artist, Warren Rapozo, painted Edward's signature logo art, which is reminiscent of the 1940 Matson line of art depicting Hawaiian women with leis, fruit and flowers in rich vibrant colors.

To get to Edward's, from Highway 11 or Ali`i Drive, turn toward the ocean on Kamehameha III; then turn right on Manukai Street. Follow to the end; then ask at the information booth at Kanaloa Condominiums.

Breakfast: $5.00–11.00, lunch: $7.00–13.00, dinner entrées: $17.00–32.00. Reservations and guest pass required, call (808)322-1434. Open daily.

Find out more about Edward's on the internet: www.edwardsatkanaloa.com.

Check out Edward's new restaurant: The Point at Kona Coast in the Kona Coast Resort, which features ethnically diverse cuisine and local specials in a casual atmosphere.

EDWARD'S BOUILLABAISSE

4 fresh fish fillets, 3 oz. each
4 fresh U12 shrimp, cleaned and deveined
12 New Zealand green lip mussels
4 cold water lobster claws
8 fresh ocean scallops
20 live Pacific clams
12 snow crab claws
4 tsp. garlic, minced
4 medium shallots, cleaned and julienne
¾ cup rich fish stock

¾ cup white cooking wine
4 tsp. Worcestershire sauce
herbs de Provence to taste
fresh basil chiffinade to taste
Spanish saffron to taste
fresh orange zest to taste
sea salt to taste
fresh ground white pepper to taste
4 tsp. whole grain Dijon mustard
light olive oil

In a deep sauté pan, add olive oil. On medium high heat, bring olive oil to smoke point. Place herbs de Provence and shallots in sauté pan; cook until half done. Place fish in pan and sear on both sides; then add all seafood and the rest of ingredients. Cover pan and bring to a hard boil; then reduce heat and cook on low heat until seafood is done and clams are open. Adjust seasoning and serve with lots of fresh warm French bread.

Makes 4 servings.

FRESH SALMON AND SHRIMP AGEAN

8 fresh salmon fillets, 3 oz. each
8 fresh U12 shrimp, cleaned and deveined
4 medium shallots, cleaned and julienne
6 oz. roasted red pepper purée
4 artichoke hearts cut in quarters
   (canned is OK)
¼ cup rich fish stock
¼ cup white cooking wine
4 tsp. Worcestershire sauce

herbs de Provence to taste
fresh basil chiffinade to taste
½ cup ultra pasteurized whipping cream
sea salt to taste
fresh ground white pepper to taste
light olive oil
flour
angel hair pasta

Dredge both sides of salmon fillets in all purpose flour, making sure to remove all loose flour. Heat sauté pan over high heat adding enough olive oil to cover bottom of pan; heat oil to smoke point. Place salmon and shrimp in pan; sauté until done (do not over cook). Remove salmon and shrimp from pan; place in a warm place until sauce is made. Add shallots and cook half-way; add the rest of ingredients. Cook sauce until it reduces by half or until slightly thick. Adjust seasoning and serve with angle hair pasta that has been tossed with olive oil and herb de Provence.

*B*eginning with the serene pond and small waterfall as you enter the restaurant, Hakone, designed to create a tranquil setting, is a study in precision. The well-ordered dining room is accented with tropical plants and flowers, shoji screens and a garden setting that can be seen through the large glass windows and doors.

Hakone features both a Sushi Bar and a Saketini Bar, where you can indulge in a Japanese "Martini" made with sake of which there are several different kinds. At our table, we tried a Sake Flight Sampler and sipped four different types of chilled sake.

With attentive and gracious service, you can enjoy a complete dinner or experience Hakone's fascinating buffet. The Crispy Soft Shell Crab Hand Roll Sushi gives a sample of incredible flavors and the artistic and sensitive attention to detail of the Sushi Chef. The buffet is an obvious hit with everyone including Japanese visitors, and features an extensive selection of Japanese dishes (and a few local Hawai'i items). The Kani (Crab Legs) are wonderful and it's great fun to try so many interesting items: Asari Sakamushi (Steamed Manila Clams), Yakizakana (Broiled Salmon and Miso Butterfish), Makizushi (Sushi Roll), `Ahi Yamakaki (Sashimi), Dim Sum and Osozai (Steamed Dumplings and assorted Japanese complements). A variety of desserts is included in the buffet; the Lilikoi Cheesecake and Almond Pound Cake are both delicious.

Complete dinners are served with plenty of side dishes, including mlso soup, steamed rice and dessert.

Buffet: $49.00; for ages 5–12 $23.00. Complete dinners: $32.00–37.00. Open five nights. Call for reservations.

TEMPURA ENTREE

12 each – 21/25 PDQ shrimp
4 pieces of snapper or other fish, 2 oz. each
4 asparagus stalks
4 small broccoli florets
4 Kabo Cha pumpkin slices
4 – ¼" slices of zucchini

2 Tbsp. daikon, grated
6 oz. dashi (Japanese soup stock)
1½ oz. mirin
1½ oz. soy sauce
flour, as needed

TEMPURA BATTER

4 cups tempura flour mix*
2 cups cold water

2 egg yolks
4–5 cups cotton seed oil

Combine flour mix, egg yolk and cold water. Set aside. Heat oil in heavy pot to approximately 350 degrees. For the sauce combine dashi, mirin and soy sauce. Warm over low flame and set aside. Dredge shrimp and vegetables in flour, shake excess off. Continue by dipping each piece in tempura batter and fry in hot oil until golden in color and cooked through. Arrange seafood and vegetables attractively on 4 dinner plates. Garnish with 1½ teaspoons grated daikon and serve tempura sauce on the side.

NEW YORK STEAK WITH PONZU SAUCE

4 prime New York strip steaks, 8 oz. each
4 types of seasonal vegetables, 2 oz. each
(haricot vert; carrot, cauliflower or asparagus)
4 oz. Maui onion, julienne

1 cup total red, yellow and green bell pepper, julienne
salt and white pepper to taste
vegetable oil
green onion for garnish

PONZU SAUCE

4 oz. citric seasoning sauce*
4 oz. soy sauce
4 Tbsp. shaved bonito flakes*

3 Tbsp. green onion, julienne
2 Tbsp. daikon, grated
½ tsp. chili paste

Combine ponzu sauce ingredients. After two hours, strain bonito flakes and set aside. Heat sauté pan, add oil as needed. Season and gently place steaks in the hot pan, turn over once during cooking to desired doneness. Let steaks rest 3 to 4 minutes. While steaks are resting, steam vegetables and divide among 4 dinner plates. Slice steak and arrange on dinner plate. Combine daikon with chili paste and garnish the steaks. Sauté onion and peppers. Season and place on top of steaks. Sprinkle with julienne green onion. Serve ponzu sauce on the side.

*Available at Asian grocery stores or Asian section in most supermarkets.

Chef Hideo Kurihara

*O*ver thirty years ago, Huggo and his wife, Shirley, started **Huggo's** restaurant as a casual and friendly place where local fishermen met to "talk story." Today, Huggo's is still in the family with their son Eric as proprietor, and it's still in the same stellar over-the-ocean location, and is continuing to be a favorite in Hawai'i—Huggo's received the 2000 Restaurant-of-Distinction Hale 'Aina Award.

Sitting in the open-air atmosphere at Huggo's—with the wooden floors and nautical theme—looking out over the clear turquoise water feels similar to being on a boat except it doesn't rock and roll, that is until the live entertainment and dancing begins each evening. In this location, you would expect the freshest fish to be served, and each day Huggo's offers a large selection of fresh fish depending on what the fishermen caught that day.

Specialties include: Coconut Kiwi Ono and Blackened 'Ahi with cucumber tomato salsa and mango aioli. Huggo's also has plenty to please meat-eaters and vegetarians, including Gourmet Island Pizzas and Certified Angus Beef. Save room for dessert. It's hard not to gasp a breathy "WOW" when one of their magnificent slices of ice cream pie is served. They offer many exotic tropical drinks from the popular Mai Tai to "Da Green Flash" or "Jungle Juice." Huggo's is friendly, fun and fresh—from the ocean air to the fish!

Lunch, Monday through Friday, $6.95-14.95. Dinner nightly, entrées $16.95–29.95.

On Kailua Bay just off Ali'i Drive (south end of the main drag). Reservations recommended for the dining room.

HUGGO'S

(808) 329-1493 • 75-5828 Kahakai Road, Kailua–Kona, Hawai'i 96740

BLACKENED AHI WITH MANGO AIOLI AND CUCUMBER TOMATO SALSA

4 `ahi steaks, 6–8 oz. each
½ cup paprika
1 Tbsp. garlic powder

1 Tbsp. cayenne pepper
1 Tbsp. black pepper
1 Tbsp. white pepper

Mix all spices well and sprinkle `ahi steaks on both sides. Prepare aioli and salsa. Sear `ahi quickly on both sides (medium rare) on a hot dry skillet. Place Mango Aioli and Cucumber Salsa on top of fish.

Serving idea: Arrange the fish on a plate with soba noodles and stir fried vegetables garnished with lemon wedges and sprigs of fresh cilantro.

MANGO AIOLI

⅓ cup fresh mango juice
1 cup mayonnaise

1 Tbsp. garlic, minced

Mix all ingredients together.

CUCUMBER TOMATO SALSA

1 cucumber
1 tomato
½ onion
1 Tbsp. fresh dill

1 Tbsp. Tabasco
salt and pepper to taste
1 Tbsp. red vinegar
1 Tbsp. olive oil

Peel cucumber and remove seeds from tomato. Dice and mix with chopped onions. Add rest of ingredients and toss together.

GRILLED ONO WITH COCONUT KIWI SAUCE AND TROPICAL FRUIT RELISH

4 ono fillets, 6–8 oz. each

Season ono fillets with salt and pepper on both sides. Grill fish to medium. Top fillet with sauce and relish, and accompany with pilaf and asparagus or broccoli, if desired.

COCONUT KIWI SAUCE

1 – 8 oz. can coconut milk
1 Tbsp. chili sambol
1 Tbsp. chicken base
⅓ cup sherry wine
1 Tbsp. ginger, minced

3 kiwi fruit, peeled and puréed
½ cup heavy cream
⅓ cup lemon juice
cornstarch

Mix coconut milk, chili sambol, chicken base, sherry and ginger together. Bring to a boil to reduce. Add puréed kiwi and reduce for 2–3 minutes. Add cream and lemon juice. Thicken with cornstarch to desired consistency.

TROPICAL FRUIT RELISH

1 cup pineapple, diced
½ cup mango, peeled and diced
½ cup kiwi, peeled and diced
⅓ cup red pepper, diced

¼ cup pickled ginger, minced
¼ cup green onions, diced
⅓ cup lime juice

All fruit can be diced to ⅛–¼". Toss gently and add lemon juice and pickled ginger.

A stroll from the Hilton lobby to Imari is like walking through a wing of an art museum and shows off only part of their impressive art collection. When you see lovely Japanese-tea-room style buildings and a tranquil pond with water lilies and koi fish, you will know that you have arrived at Imari. Once inside, you'll be greeted by kimonos, Japanese music, black-lacquer furnishings and a choice of which kind of dining experience you'd like to have.

The teppanyaki chefs are talented in both the culinary arts and the performing arts creating a lively, entertaining and incredibly delicious experience. There's a sense of comraderie as you sit around the grill with other guests all watching with anticipation as your meals are prepared and served with so much flair and care. The Hawaiian Lobster (recommended by the chef) is outstanding and my favorite veggie is by far the Maui Onions—so sweet and flavorful!

Sushi lovers will be pleased by the excellent sushi bar. Or, try an assortment of sushi served as a dinner in the dining room. If you're not quite ready for raw fish, try the Samurai Maki Sushi dinner: rolled sushi that includes Maine lobster, softshell crab, jumbo shrimp, and California maki. Shabu–shabu, also available, is a traditional Japanese dining experience served table-side and set over an open-flame burner at your table. Dinners are served with miso shiru, steamed rice and Japanese green tea.

Dinner: $28.00–49.00. A la carte sushi: $4.50–15.00. Call for reservations and nights open.

LOBSTER DYNAMITE

8 oz. lobster meat

16 shiitake mushrooms, sliced

1 pound yellow onion, sliced

1 oz. tobiko roe

3 slices avocado

Prepare sauce, then sauté lobster meat, sliced shiitake mushrooms and yellow onion. Pour sauce on top of lobster and put under broiler for 4–5 minutes to perfect. Then lay avocado on top of sauce and put under broiler for another 30 seconds. Place tobiko on top.

DYNAMITE SAUCE

1 cup mayonnaise

1 egg yolk

salt and pepper to taste

Mix all ingredients together.

MAGURO TATAKI

1 pound `ahi block

1 Tbsp. Hawaiian red salt

1 Tbsp. Japanese chili peppers

For Garnish:

1 Tbsp. green onions, chopped

1 oz. momiji oroshi

1 oz. daikon, grated

1 tsp. chili paste

2 slices of lemon

Put salt and chili pepper on the outside of the `ahi block. Set for 15 minutes. Grill each side for 2–3 minutes evenly, then place in refrigerator to cool. Cut in ⅛" slices, garnish and serve with ponzu sauce.

PONZU SAUCE

3 oz. rice vinegar

3 oz. shoyu (soy) sauce

3 oz. citrus juice

Mix all ingredients together.

Chef Nobuyuki Atsumi

The four incredibly diverse and equally wonderful restaurants I've included from the Hilton Waikoloa Village all give you an opportunity to enjoy the fantasyland created there. With enough time before your dinner reservation, you can enjoy sinking into the tropical wonder of pools, gardens, and waterfalls while meandering along paths and bridges to get to your destination. If you want a speedier way of life (and your timing is right—on 10 minute intervals), catch the tram from the lobby. For a more leisurely and certainly more romantic ride, catch the boat. This is a nice way to end the evening—floating peacefully under the stars. **Kamuela Provision Company** serves fresh and fabulous food in a perfect contemporary Hawaiian setting that is elegant yet casual, open-air and lovely. Reserve a table on the lanai if you want to be steps from the ocean and under the stars while listening to the live solo guitarist. If you're there for the exquisite Hawaiian sunset, you'll see a buffed-out young man in a sarong run by to light the tiki torches and another will blow the conch shell. It's quite a treat while sipping your tropical Mai Tai, Piña Colada or cocktail of choice.

Local fresh ingredients are used whenever possible with an emphasis on clean healthy flavors. The Pacific Style Bouillabaisse is recommended, and the Volcano Spiced Charred `Ahi is soooo delicious! Or the Macadamia Nut Crusted Fish—great flavors. If you can't decide which decadent dessert you'd like, they offer a dessert sampler.

Dinner only. $24.00–44.00. Call for reservations and nights open.

KAMUELA PROVISION COMPANY

(808) 886-1234 ext. 2892 • Hilton Waikoloa Village, Waikoloa, Hawai'i 96738

GRILLED ASIAN MARINATED LAMB

16 lamb chops cut from rack, 1 bone each
3 oz. honey
3 oz. mustard
3 oz. shoyu (soy sauce)

2 Tbsp. ginger, minced
3 Tbsp. sesame oil
2 Tbsp. garlic, minced

Mix well and marinate lamb overnight or for a minimum of 4 hours. Grill to desired temperature. Serve with garlic mashed potatoes, fresh corn and pineapple mint chutney.

PINEAPPLE MINT CHUTNEY

1 oz. salad oil
2 oz. onions, diced
1½ oz. red bell pepper, diced
½ large pineapple, diced
2 oz. sugar

2 oz. rice vinegar
1 Tbsp. ginger, grated
1 stick cinnamon
fresh mint, chopped

Sauté onion in oil until tender. Add remaining ingredients and a third of the mint. Cook until reduced and slightly thickened. Adjust seasoning and consistency. Cool before adding remaining mint. Chill well.

STEAMED PACIFIC CLAMS WITH RED CURRY AIOLI

40 clams, hard shell type, wash free of sand
2 oz. Chardonnay wine
¼ cup leeks, julienne very fine
¼ cup carrots, julienne very fine
2 Tbsp. garlic, minced

4 oz. clam stock or juice
2 oz. butter
fresh ground black pepper to taste
2 Tbsp. parsley, chopped fine
additional carrots and parsley for garnish

Add all ingredients in a small pot with lid and bring to a boil. Give an occasional shake until all clams are open, approximately 3–5 minutes. Put 10 clams in each bowl. Distribute sauce evenly; garnish with Red Curry Aioli, carrots and parsley. (Aioli can also be served on croutons.)

Serves 4.

RED CURRY AIOLI

1 egg yolk
1 tsp. garlic
1 tsp. red curry paste

salt to taste
1 oz. lemon juice
1¼ cups olive oil

In a blender, add egg yolk, garlic, curry and salt. Run machine slowly and alternate pouring olive oil and lemon until thick (if too thick, add some water).

Chef James Babian

*C*lose to the barren landscape of Kilauea Volcano, Volcano Village is lush and often misty, with immense ferns and other amazing over-sized plants. In the midst of this mystical place, Kilauea Lodge offers a cozy retreat to warm you inside and out. People from all over the world have come to the historic "International Fireplace of Friendship" in the Lodge, which was built in 1938. Many children have been inspired by the Volcano during the day and awed by Pele myths told by the warm fire in the evenings.

Owners Chef Albert and Lorna Jeyte offer romantic overnight accommodations that include a complimentary full breakfast. Before his debut as a talented chef, Albert was an Emmy award-winning make-up artist.

With lots of wood, fresh flowers, and beautiful original watercolors painted on silk, Kilauea Lodge offers a warm and charming atmosphere for enjoying the exceptional dinner entrées and nightly specials: Seafood Mauna Kea—a combination of seafood and mushrooms sautéed in a creme fraiche sauce with shallots and fresh basil, served atop a bed of fettucine and rainbow rotelles, Leg of Antelope Fillet or Medallions of Venison.

Open nightly. Full dinners (includes soup and salad) range from $16.00–43.00. Call for reservations. Located one mile from Volcanoes National Park in Volcano Village.

POISSON CRUX
(TAHITIAN STYLE CEVICHE)

1 pound mahimahi or ono (wahoo tuna)

1 tsp. rock salt

4 large limes, squeezed

1 cup coconut milk (frozen or canned)

½ cup carrots, grated

½ cup celery, finely chopped

Cut fish into 1″ cubes. Marinate with salt and lime juice. Massage salt and lime juice into the fish. Let stand for 1 hour covered on the kitchen counter. Lightly drain mixture. Add coconut milk, carrots and celery. Serve cold on lettuce leaves.

BROILED MAHIMAHI WITH MANGO–CHUTNEY SAUCE AND MACADAMIA NUTS

8 – 8 oz. pieces mahimahi

butter, softened

½ cup macadamia nuts, chopped

chopped parsley for garnish

Prepare the sauce. Brush both sides of the fish with butter and broil on both sides until cooked and slightly brown. Place the fish on serving dishes and spoon 3 teaspoons of the sauce over the middle of each. Sprinkle the nuts over the sauce and top with parsley.

MANGO–CHUTNEY SAUCE

2 cups mango chutney

3 oz. white Chablis wine

2 Tbsp. cider vinegar

6 Tbsp. packed brown sugar

1 oz. sherry

½ tsp. white pepper

¼ cup lilikoi or guava juice (optional)

¼ cup pineapple juice

In blender or processor, purée the mango chutney until smooth and creamy. Pour the chutney into a medium saucepan and add the sauce ingredients. Stir over low to moderate heat. Reduce the heat and simmer for 10 minutes, stirring frequently. Keep the sauce warm.

*C*hinese antiques and hand made items, including beautiful wall hangings that are hand embroidered and a hand-painted mural from China, add an authentic air to **Kirin** and complement the authentic Chinese cuisine. The chefs are from China and Hong Kong and are not influenced by the local style. Their live seafood specialties are highly recommended; they even have a tank of live fish in the kitchen. That's fresh!

As our table filled up with many delicious treats, I sat back in awe admiring the exquisitely beautiful presentation and intricate attention to detail. The star was the Peppery Salt Dungeness Crab (they offer 5 different preparations) with a flavor so out-standing it's addictive! Or, try the Open-flame roasted Peking Duck. Dim Sum is always a treat (and not easily found outside of metropolitan areas) and is served at lunch and all afternoon as well. It is perfect for those of us who love to enjoy many delightful and tasty little packages of food.

For enhanced romance in the evening, reserve a table on their outdoor balcony where you'll have candle-light and a view of the lagoon and the ocean's white waves lit up from the moon against the dark night.

Kirin is located above Donatoni's. Ala carte items: $4.00-25.00. Lunch and dinner. Call for days open and reservations.

GENERAL TSAO CHICKEN

8 oz. chicken breast, cut in ⅜" slices	1½ Tbsp. cornstarch
1 oz. light soy sauce	2½ cups peanut oil

This is a spicy sweet and sour dish. A very hot wok is necessary. Mix soy sauce, cornstarch and sliced chicken breast. Heat oil in wok until smoking hot; add chicken and fry until light brown. Drain oil and set aside. Set chicken aside and return wok to burner. When wok is smoking, add 1 tablespoon of the drained peanut oil and the following ingredients and stir fry.

4 oz. bamboo shoots, sliced thin	½ bell pepper, cubed
4 oz. carrots, sliced thin	1 Tbsp. red jalapeno, sliced and deseeded
4 oz. shiitake mushroom, sliced as thick as the chicken	1 tsp. garlic, minced

When almost done, add the following ingredients and thicken with cornstarch slurry.

1 tsp. chili sauce (sambol)	1½ Tbsp. sugar
¼ cup Chinkiang vinegar	

"Jun Tong Tsao was a brilliant general in the Ching Dynasty. At retirement to his hometown, the emperor rewarded him with an entourage of chefs, servants and maids to serve him the rest of his life.

One of the chefs was excellent at cooking a sliced chicken dish that was tangy and spicy, which was appetizing to the general's taste. The general loved it so much that he ordered the kitchen to serve it at every dinner.

In Chinese lore, General Tsao was a respected man (Yee duck Fook Yun) for his honesty and fairness."

BACON ROLL

½ strip bacon	light soy sauce
1 shrimp (31/36) peeled and deveined	white pepper
1 scallop (med) cleaned	peanut oil

Mix shrimp and scallop with light soy sauce and white pepper. Roll 1 shrimp and 1 scallop in ½ strip bacon. Dust roll in cornstarch and deep fry in hot peanut oil. Serve with Citrus Mayonnaise or thousand island dressing.

This recipe was developed by corporate Chef Archie Chik.

CITRUS MAYONNAISE

½ cup mayonnaise	white pepper
juice from ½ lime	dash of Worcestershire

Mix together.

For a very special treat on your way to Waipi`o Valley (or if you're anywhere near Honoka`a), make sure to stop in at Mamane Street Bakery & Café. Since 1993 the bakers of Mamane have been arriving during the wee hours of the morning to prepare scrumptious baked goods that entice people from all over the island.

In 1968 Ely Pessah, owner and pastry chef, left his home in Cairo, Egypt, and arrived in the United States where he spent years as a pastry chef in four and five-star resorts before opening this charming bakery. They now supply high quality coffee houses, restaurants and even an airline with their bakery items.

Popular breads include the Portuguese Sweet Bread and the Potato Bread. Honey Nut Bran Muffins, Orange Cranberry Scones, Fresh Fruit Tarts (beautiful and yummy!), fresh Poppyseed or Blueberry Bagels are examples of other delicious choices. They also make fabulous Focaccia—Three Cheese and Marinara Mozzarella, Ham and Cheese Croissants and some sandwiches. If you want to try fresh roasted macadamia nuts, this is the place. They roast 'em themselves.

You can get your treats to go or enjoy the quaint atmosphere and sit at one of the few small tables, while sipping a cappuccino or espresso. Open daily from 7 am through the afternoon. Under $10.00.

You can order many of their goodies on the web at mamanebakery.com.

ISLAND BANANA MACADAMIA NUT BREAD

3½ pounds bananas, very ripe

2¼ cups sugar

1 cup vegetable oil

2 large eggs

1 Tbsp. vanilla extract

3 cups flour

1 Tbsp. baking soda

½ tsp. baking powder

3 oz. macadamia nuts, diced (optional)

Peel bananas and mash very well. Add sugar, incorporate well; then add oil, eggs and vanilla. Mix all dry ingredients together and add to banana mixture. Mix well. Paper and grease 3 – 8x8x2″ pans and divide batter equally. Sprinkle nuts on top. Bake in preheated oven at 365 degrees for 30 minutes. Touch top to check if done. Will keep well if chilled. You can also freeze for later use.

ORANGE WALNUT SHORT BREAD COOKIES

1 pound butter, unsalted, soft

1½ cups powdered sugar

1 orange, rind from

1 tsp. vanilla

5½ cups all purpose flour

1 cup walnuts

Cream butter and powdered sugar in mixing bowl. Add orange rind and vanilla. Blend in flour then walnuts. Mix well. Remove from bowl and onto lined sheet pan. Press by hand until 1½″ thick. Square dough as much as possible. Cover with plastic and chill for 4 hours or longer, then cut as shown and lay flat on lined pan. Bake in preheated 360 degree oven until golden brown on edges.

"Exciting, regional, tasteful and fun," are words that Chef Peter Merriman uses to describe what a restaurant should be, and he is a master at creating exactly what he describes in his restaurants. Since 1988, Merriman's Restaurant has been luring food aficionados from all over Hawai'i and the world to enjoy delicious, creative and fresh food utilizing locally grown ingredients. Called the "Pied Piper of Hawai'i Regional Cuisine" by the *LA Times*, and "a culinary renaissance man" by the *New York Times*—Merriman has 2 exceptional award-winning

restaurants (see Hula Grill page 112) with more ventures on the way. Peter Merriman has traveled throughout North America on culinary tours representing the Hawai'i Visitor's Bureau, the Department of Agriculture and Hawaiian Airlines, and has appeared on numerous television shows.

In an ambiance that is pleasant and comfortable, you can sample Chef Merriman's notable cuisine choosing from items such as: Sesame Crusted Fresh Island Fish sautéed with spicy lilikoi sauce and tomato papaya relish; Wok Charred `Ahi; or Grilled Fresh Diver Scallops with lemongrass vinaigrette. Appetizers include Wainaku Sweet Corn and Shrimp Fritters, and Kalua Pig and Goat Cheese Quesadilla. Lunch offers a selection of creative entrées, soups and salads.

Lunch served Monday through Friday, $6.95–11.95. Dinner nightly. Entrées: $15.95–34.95. Reservations recommended.

SHRIMP AND TOMATO LINGUINI

24 pieces fresh shrimp	2 Tbsp. butter
2 Tbsp. olive oil	4 Tbsp. fresh basil, chopped
1½ cups tomato, diced	1 pound cooked linguini
¼ cup kalamata olives	salt to taste
3 Tbsp. roasted garlic, chopped	fresh ground black pepper

In a hot sauté pan, add olive oil and cook shrimp until ¾ done. Add tomatoes, olives, garlic and butter. Add linguini and basil. Toss to blend ingredients. Season to taste with salt and fresh ground pepper.

Serves 4.

PLUM PAPAYA DIPPING SAUCE

1 cup soft papaya pulp	2 tsp. fresh ginger
1 cup Chinese plum sauce	½ cup green onion
⅓ cup rice wine vinegar	½ tsp. salt
1 tsp. garlic	½ cup vegetable oil
1 tsp. shallot	

Place all ingredients but the vegetable oil in a food processor. Purée until smooth. Slowly add the vegetable oil.

Makes 3 cups. This versatile sauce can be used as a dipping sauce for shrimp, a glaze for ribs, a dressing for a vegetable slaw or fruit salad, or a sauce for fish.

When I asked Amy Ferguson Ota, executive chef and owner of the jazzy, sophisticated noodle shop, Oodles of Noodles, how she came up with the concept, she said, "I love noodles. It all came about from the love of noodles." Simple as that. Pioneer and trailblazer, she was one of the first prominent Southwestern chefs, one of the first Hawai'i Regional Cuisine chefs, the first female to be executive chef of a five-star resort at the Hotel Hana Maui and later the Ritz Carlton Mauna Lani on the Big Island.

With Amy's high standards, everything is made from scratch using the freshest ingredients, including organic greens and edible flowers (a nice touch on the already attractive presentation). A variety of ethnic flavors is artfully blended with fresh quality pasta creating dishes such as Kona Style Tuna Noodle Casserole with shiitake cream, wok seared 'ahi topped with flavorful crisp sweet onions. It's creamy and smooth and oh soo good. (Not Mom's tuna casserole!) You'll find the same creativity in a great selection of salads and soups: Spicy Pacific Caesar in Lumpia Basket and vegetarian or meat eaters versions of Oodles' Saimin. Oodles of Noodles offers each guest tremendous flexibility with lots of "add ons," plenty of vegetarian selections, options to care for special nutritional needs and more. Amy says their specialty is very simple; it's giving people what they want, exceeding expectations and making their guests happy so they want to come back. Try the special shaved ice desserts, which are beautiful, spectacular and refreshing!

Lunch: $7.95–15.95. Dinner: $8.95–21.95. Open daily. Stays open through the afternoon also. Located near Safeway. (And not related to the "Oodles of Noodles" on the Mainland.)

OODLES' SUMMER ROLL

4 large rice papers

2 oz. cooked rice noodles

4 red leaf lettuce leaves, cleaned, no rib

2 oz. carrot strings or julienne carrots

2 oz. cucumber strings or julienne

fresh herbs of choice: Thai basil, mint, cilantro, etc.

choice of sweet chili sauce, hoisin peanut sauce, spicy plum sauce

Have ready not only the above ingredients, but a pot of boiling water. Dip rice paper in hot water until pliable. Lay on flat surface and layer with lettuce leaves, rice noodles, vegetables and herbs, then fold similar to a burrito. Serve with sauce for dipping.
Serves 4.
Summer rolls are best if served immediately and if you are truly a daring hostess, have your guests make their own. It's a great party idea.

CHICKEN AND OKINAWAN SWEET POTATO THAI GREEN CURRY

2 Tbsp. peanut or vegetable oil, optional

2 cups chicken thighs, diced

2 cups Japanese eggplant, sliced

1 large sweet potato, roasted, peeled and cubed

Green Curry Sauce, use full recipe below

basil, cilantro, ginger and cumin

jasmine or sticky rice or noodles

bean sprouts, scallions, fresh herbs

Heat a large skillet over high heat with or without oil. Sauté chicken, sear and add eggplant. Once chicken is two-thirds cooked, add green curry sauce and sweet potato. Simmer until chicken and eggplant are cooked. Finish with an herb mixture containing basil, cilantro, ginger and cumin. Serve in heated soup plates with either jasmine or sticky rice or noodles. Garnish with bean sprouts, scallions, and fresh herbs.

GREEN CURRY SAUCE

5 Tbsp. green curry paste

2 Tbsp. ginger, chopped

1 Tbsp. lemongrass, chopped

2 – 13 oz. cans coconut milk

Sauté ginger, lemongrass and garlic, add coconut milk. Bring to simmer, whip green curry paste into mixture. Reduce by ⅓.

When you're in Kamuela, you're in the heart of the Big Island's ranching community and Parker Ranch Grill is just the place to experience some paniolo (cowboy) flavor! With a decor that is rich in koa and ohia woods, historical Parker Ranch photographs, a colorful collection of cowboy boots and cowhide furniture, you might just feel like breaking into a camp song. The warm hearty feeling is enhanced by large fireplaces in both the dining room and the lounge where guitars and ukuleles are waiting for a musical soul to give them life.

The menu features some old favorites and some tempting innovative choices: Ranch Style Meatloaf with sweet corn cheddar casserole; Lobster Pot Pie with local corn, shiitake mushrooms and garlic mashed potatoes; Ribsteak crusted with chilies and citrus, smoked tomato-pistachio butter. Local beef items and a Vegetable Torte round out the menu. The warm Fresh Fruit Cobbler is served in an iron skillet—another example of how the ranch theme is carried through with enormous attention to detail. (Parker Ranch Grill has their own private label wine.)

Lunch daily: $7.00–15.00.

Dinner nightly: $13.00–25.00.

PARKER RANCH GRILL'S CHICKEN POT PIE

6 oz. poached chicken, diced
1 oz. each carrots, onion, celery, diced
½ oz. button mushrooms, diced
1 oz. green peas
½ Tbsp. fresh thyme
1 cup milk

½ tsp. fresh rosemary
¼ cup melted butter
cornstarch slurry
salt and pepper to taste
puff pastry

Heat butter in a sauté pan; add carrots, celery, onions, mushrooms, and herbs. Cook until vegetables are tender, but firm. Add milk and bring to a boil. Turn down to a simmer; add peas and season with salt and pepper. Add cornstarch slurry slowly, stirring until a thick consistency is reached. Pour into serving dish and add puff pastry top.

PARKER RANCH GRILL'S FRESH FRUIT COBBLER

FILLING

2 cups mixed berries (strawberry, blueberry, raspberry)
¼ cup sugar
pinch of salt

juice of ½ lemon
½ oz. butter
⅓ cup water
cornstarch slurry

Put half of the berries into a heavy pot with the sugar and salt. Slowly bring the mixture to a boil, and cook until the berries become juicy and a thick jam-like sauce forms. Add the remaining berries, lemon juice and butter. Cook just until the mixture comes to a boil and add cornstarch slurry to thicken. Remove from heat and cool. Filling is complete.

CRUMBLE TOPPING

1½ cups flour
½ cup sugar

5 oz. butter

Run ingredients together in a mixer. Mixture should look like corn meal. Add fruit filling to a seasoned iron skillet. Crumble topping over pie, make thick enough to create a crust. Bake in a preheated oven at 350 degrees for 12 minutes. Serve warm with Tahitian vanilla bean ice cream.

"I wish you'd open a Sibu Café where I live." These are words Peter Weinstock, the owner Sibu Café hears often. Since 1982, this fabulous little gem has been pleasing customers with unique and exotic Indonesian food; some items are traditional such as Shrimp Laska—shrimp, baby corn, green beans, rice noodles & bean sprouts in a fragrant sauce made with coconut milk, lemongrass and Indonesian spices. They also serve their own popular originals—Garlic Shrimp with Linguini and a sauce made with garlic, basil, parsley, cilantro, ripe tomatoes, black pepper and green chilies. Also, Beef, Chicken, Vegetable or Shrimp Saté and many more great selections, including lots of choice vegetarian entrées are on the menu. All food is prepared without MSG or white sugar.

Sibu features a short international beer and wine list, which is carefully chosen to complement the spicy flavorful food. Sibu Café is relaxed and casual with a few tables inside where interesting masks adorn the walls; some are 50–60 years old and were brought back with Peter from his travels to Indonesia. Or, you can sit in the courtyard area shown in the illustration.

Sibu Café is tucked away in the Banyan Court Mall across from the sea wall (where the waves sometimes splash over onto the road). There is a parking lot behind Sibu Café; just turn on Lakani Street (one–way) and you'll find it. Lunch and dinner served daily. $8.95–13.95. No credit cards.

SIBU CAFE

(808) 329-1112 • 75-5695 Ali'i Drive, Kailua–Kona, Hawai'i 96740

PINEAPPLE CURRY

8 oz. pineapple, cubed
1 Tbsp. oil
1 small onion, finely chopped
1 tsp. garlic, minced
1 small stick cinnamon
3 whole cloves
3 cardamom pods, bruised

1 Tbsp. coriander
1 ½ tsp. cumin
½ tsp. sambal oelek
1 tsp. salt
1 cup coconut milk
1 tsp. dark brown sugar

Heat oil. Fry onion, garlic and whole spices over medium heat. Stir frequently until onion is soft. Add coriander, cumin, sambal oelek and salt. Fry for a few minutes until spices are browned. Add pineapple and stir well to coat each piece with the spice mixture. Add coconut milk and sugar. Bring to a simmer, stirring constantly. Simmer for a few more minutes until pineapple softens. Serve and enjoy.

NASI KUNIT – FRAGRANT YELLOW RICE

2 cups uncooked white rice
2 cups water
1 cup coconut milk
1 tsp. salt
½ tsp. turmeric

3 keffir lime leaves
3 pieces fresh lemongrass root, bruised
optional: ½ tsp. Laos powder, Kencur powder, or good quality cardamom for additional fragrance.

Aggressively rinse the rice until the water is clear. Mix the water, coconut milk, salt, turmeric and any other fragrant spices using a whisk. Add the lemongrass and the lime leaves. Cook the rice in this mixture. Remove the lemongrass and the lime leaves; fluff before serving.

> *"Perfectly simple—and simply perfect. This is the dish friends request that I bring to all the pot lucks. This is true."* — Peter Weinstock

INDONESIAN & SOUTHEAST ASIAN KAILUA–KONA, HAWAIʻI

When you're exploring Volcano National Park and you're ready for a nice place to relax and enjoy a fine meal, you'll be pleased to discover Surt's at Volcano Village. Executive Chef Surt Thammountha has combined talents with owners Brian and Lisha Crawford to offer "quality and gourmet flavors at a reasonable price." Lisha explains that everything is made from scratch using fresh ingredients and, she confides, the secret is in the sauce, which takes hours to prepare. That must be why they are touted as "the newest taste sensation in Volcano Village." Surt's is small and cozy with open beam ceilings, soft track lighting, classical or Hawaiian music and white linen table cloths. Photographs of the volcano by Brad Lewis, and original oil paintings by Marion Berger grace the wood-paneled walls.

An appetizer specialty to try is: Angel Wings, boneless chicken wings stuffed with vegetables and noodles. Surt's offers a variety of Asian and European specialties, such as Vegetarian Curry, Beef Panang, Pasta Primavera, Lobster Ravioli and more. Each day the chef prepares specials such as: Opah (Moonfish) with a light Thai Crab Curry Butter Sauce. I tried the Seafood Fettucinni—'ahi, calamari and shrimp with a delectably rich and flavorful cream sauce. You may enjoy a bottle of wine or beer from their carefully considered list, and how about Mango Tiramisu for dessert? Yum.

Lunch entrées: $7.95–14.95, served noon to 4 pm. Dinner entrées: $11.95–24.95, from 4 to 9:30 pm. Dinner reservations recommended. Open daily.

Look for Surt's on the Beach on the North shore of Kaua'i, where lunch and dinner are served daily in an ocean-front location. (808) 826-0060.

CHICKEN CARBONARA

2 oz. oil

2 chicken breasts

4 oz. chopped bacon

2 tsp. garlic, chopped

2 oz. onion, chopped

7 oz. mushrooms, sliced

2 oz. tomato, diced

white wine

salt to taste

12 oz. cream sauce

20 oz. linguine

3 oz. powdered parmesan cheese

2 tsp. parsley, chopped

Pour oil into hot pan. Drop chicken breasts into hot oil, add a pinch of salt, turn over then place in oven to keep warm. Add bacon to pan and sauté until golden brown. Add garlic, onion, mushrooms, tomato, mix all together and sauté with white wine. Combine with cooked linguine, cream sauce, parmesan cheese and parsley. Place in center of plates; then cut each chicken breast into 5 strips and place around top of pasta mixture.

BEEF PANANG

1 oz. oil

8 oz. onions, chopped

1 tsp. garlic, chopped

12 oz. peas

16 oz. beef, sliced

red curry paste, to taste

12 leaves of fresh basil

4–8 broken up lime leaves

8 oz. stock

24 oz. coconut milk

8 oz. Thai peanut sauce

2 oz. white shoyu (soy sauce)

8 tsp. fish sauce

2 tsp. sugar

Pour oil into hot pan. Add onions and garlic, sauté; then add peas, beef, red curry paste, basil and lime leaves. Mix all together. Add rest of ingredients and let it reduce down until mixture thickens. Serve in bowls with a serving of rice.

`Ahi — very popular, often served as sashimi. `Ahi is the Hawaiian name for yellowfin and bigeye tuna. It is red in color when raw and turns almost white when cooked.

Aku — also known as skipjack tuna, and may be eaten raw as sashimi or cooked.

Bok Choy — a Chinese cabbage with dark green leaves and a white stem.

Cilantro* — Chinese parsley.

Coconut Milk* — made from coconut meat and water. Available canned or frozen.

Daikon* — in the turnip family with a similar flavor to a radish.

Dashi* — Japanese soup stock.

Fish Sauce* — a thick, brown, salty sauce made from anchovies.

Furikake* — a Japanese seasoning mix of dried seaweed and sesame seeds.

Ginger — a rhizome (similar to a root). Peel the outer skin, then finely chop or grate. It has a spicy flavor.

Green Papaya — see Papaya.

Guava — a plum size tropical fruit primarily used for juices, jellies and sauces.

Hoisin Sauce* — a sweet , spicy, fermented soybean sauce.

Jicama — a root similar to a turnip. Crunchy and flavorful raw. Can also be cooked.

Kaffir Lime Leaves* — often used in Thai cooking, they produce a citrus flavor and aroma.

Kiawe Wood — similar to mesquite.

Lehi — a delicately flavored pink snapper.

Lemongrass — long greenish-gray stalks that add a lemony flavor to dishes.

Lilikoi* — passion fruit. Available in frozen concentrate form, which is often used in recipes.

Lumpia* — used to wrap egg rolls and other items.

Lychee — a delicious fruit with soft, sweet, juicy meat surrounded by a reddish woody shell that needs to be removed before eating the fruit.

Mahimahi — dolphin fish (unrelated to the mammal). White, delicately flavored meat. Very popular.

Mango — a sweet tropical fruit that is yellow with some orange and red. In some recipes peaches my be used as a substitute.

Maui Onion — a sweet and mild onion grown in the cooler climate of Kula, the upcountry region of Maui.

Mirin* — a sweetened rice wine. One teaspoon of sugar may be substituted for one teaspoon of Mirin.

Miso* — a thick fermented soybean paste commonly used to make miso soup, which is light and brothy.

Mongchong — a moist, mild and tender fish.

Nori* — sheets of dried, compressed seaweed used for wrapping sushi rolls.

Onaga — a delicately flavored red snapper. Snapper, monkfish and orange roughy may be substituted for onaga.

Ono/Wahoo — similar to mackerel or tuna with white, delicate, flaky meat. Often used as a substitute for mahimahi.

Opah/Moonfish — pink to orange flesh. Suitable for a variety of preparations.

Opakapaka — Hawaiian pink snapper with a delicate flavor and moist meat. Snapper may be used as a substitute.

Panko* — crispy Japanese bread crumbs used for breading.

Papaya — a very popular pear shaped fruit with yellow skin when ripe. The melon-like flesh is sweet and mild. When used unripe, it is called green papaya and is usually shredded for salads.

Papio — a flaky, tender white fish with a mild flavor.

Poke — pieces of raw fish in a flavorful marinade including seaweed and sesame oil.

Pupu — appetizer, hors d' oeuvre.

Sake* — Japanese rice wine.

Sambal Olek — red chili paste.

Sashimi — thin slices of extremely fresh raw salt water fish. `Ahi is most commonly used for sashimi.

Shichimi — a Japanese spice blend.

Shiitake Mushrooms* — large mushrooms with dark caps. Available dried or fresh.

Shoyu/Soy Sauce* — a salty liquid flavoring made from soybeans.

Taro — a tuberous vegetable. Taro is a staple food of the Hawaiian culture and is used to make poi (a thick starchy paste). The flesh is a light purplish-gray. Taro is now being used by many chefs in a way similar to potatoes (chips, hash browns, etc.).

Tobiko* — often used in sushi, it is the orange-redish roe of the flying fish.

Tofu — white soybean curd with a mild flavor. Blocks of tofu, which are packed in water (drain and rinse tofu before using) are available in most supermarkets.

Uku — gray snapper.

Wasabi* — similar to horseradish. May be purchased in powder form and mixed with water to make a paste. Served with sushi.

*May be found in Asian food stores or the Asian section of most supermarkets.

G

H, I

RECIPE INDEX

Note: Chefs and restaurant owners chose the recipes that they wished to contribute. Some represent items from the menu, others are specials that are served occasionally or seasonally.

The recipes have not been kitchen tested by the author. Effort has been made to make the recipes clear and easy to follow and they have been proofread three times. Be adventuresome, experiment and enjoy!

RESTAURANT INDEX

Grandma's Coffee House (Featured on page 110.)

153 Kula Highway, Keokea, Maui, Hawai`i 96790

1-800-375-7853   808-878-2140   **grandmascoffee.com**

Organic Hawaiian grown coffees.

Hawai`i Regional Cuisine Marketplace (Featured on page 80.)

Liberty House at Ala Moana, 4th Floor, Honolulu, Hawai`i 96814

808-945-8888

Assorted coffees, mac nut oil blend and other flavored oils, preserves, condiments and cookies.

Hawaiian Vintage Chocolate Company

4614 Kilauea Avenue, Suite 435, Honolulu, Hawai`i 96816

808-735-8494   **hawaiianchocolate.com**

Vintage chocolates made from chocolate grown on the Big Island of Hawai`i.

Kalaheo Coffee Company & Café (Featured on page 40.)

2-2426 Kaumualii Highway, #A-2, Kalaheo, Kaua`i, Hawai`i 96741

1-800-255-0137   808-332-5858   **kalaheo.com**

Hawaiian grown and international coffees.

Mamane Street Bakery & Café (Featured on page 178.)

Mamane Street, Honoka`a, Hawai`i 96727

808-775-9478   **mamanebakery.com**

Coffee, fresh roasted macadamia nuts, Hawaiian Sweet Bread, Hawaiian gourmet butters,
jams, jellies, chutney and honey.

Maui Jelly Factory

1464 Lower Main Street, Suite 104, Wailuku, Maui, Hawai`i 96793

1-800-803-8343   808-242-6989   Fax 808-242-8389

Jams, jellies, mustards, sauces, syrups, salad dressings and candies.

Take Home Maui, Inc.

121 Dickenson Street, Lahaina, Maui, Hawai`i 96761

1-800-545-MAUI   808-661-8067   Fax 808-661-1550

Maui grown pineapples, Maui onions, papayas, macadamia nuts.

To order more copies of

Tasting Paradise

Restaurants & Recipes of the Hawaiian Islands

SECOND EDITION

Send $18.95 per book plus $3.50 for shipping and handling.

(Shipping includes up to 10 books per address.)

Coastal
IMPRESSIONS
PRESS, LLC
P.O. Box 1006
Kula, HI 96790-1006

*Remember they make great gifts for cooking and
traveling friends. Bon Appétit!*

To order more copies of

Tasting Paradise

Restaurants & Recipes of the Hawaiian Islands

SECOND EDITION

Send $18.95 per book plus $3.50 for shipping and handling.

(Shipping includes up to 10 books per address.)

Coastal
IMPRESSIONS
PRESS, LLC
P.O. Box 1006
Kula, HI 96790-1006

Remember they make great gifts for cooking and
traveling friends. Bon Appétit!